THE HOMEBREW JOURNAL

From Ingredients to Glass

AN ESSENTIAL RECORD OF RECIPES AND OBSERVATIONS

Ben Keene

First published in 2014 by Voyageur Press, a member of Quayside Publishing Group,
400 First Avenue North, Suite 400, Minneapolis, MN, 55401 USA

ISBN: 978-0-7603-4589-4

Library of Congress Cataloging-in-Publication Data

Keene, Ben, 1978-
The homebrew journal / Ben Keene.
pages cm
Includes bibliographical references and index.
ISBN 978-0-7603-4589-4 (hardcover : alk. paper)
1. Brewing–Amateurs' manuals. I. Title.
TP570.K423 2014
641.87'3–dc23
2013036405

Design Manager: James Kegley
Design & Layout: Danielle Smith

Special thanks to Justin Walsh.

Printed in China

10 9 8 7 6 5 4 3 2 1

CONTENTS

INTRODUCTION

Welcome to the club. If you didn't already think of yourself as a homebrewer, treat this journal as your de facto membership card. As of 2012, there were an estimated 1 million homebrewers throughout the United States, approximately 37,000 of whom are members of the American Homebrewers Association. A hobby enjoyed on an individual basis as well as a popular cooperative activity, homebrewing is now officially legal in all fifty states, where more than 1,500 groups meet regularly to compare notes, judge each other's beers, and learn more about the craft.

Although outlawed in the United States in 1919 when the federal government enacted Prohibition, homebrewing has deep roots in American history. Many of the country's Founding Fathers, including George Washington and Thomas Jefferson, brewed their own beer. Before the practice was legalized again by President Jimmy Carter in 1978, the Maltose Falcons of Los Angeles, California, became the nation's first homebrew club in 1974.

Ten years later, after launching the American Homebrewers Association (and *Zymurgy* magazine) with Charlie Matzen, engineer Charlie Papazian published *The Complete Joy of Homebrewing*, a book that has been revised twice but has remained in print ever since. Flash forward to the present, and there's now a National Homebrew Day (the first Saturday in May), a national competition that draws thousands of entries year after year, and supply shops from coast to coast. The number of resources now available to the beginner, intermediate, or advanced homebrewer is staggering, as is the sophistication of the equipment used and the quality of the beer produced. That said, homebrewing remains a fun, affordable (basic kits typically cost less than $60), and easy-to-learn hobby. Lest you think it's beyond your capabilities, just remember that old chestnut: brewers make wort, yeast makes beer. In other words, if you're worried about mastering the process right away, just imagine the microorganisms doing most of the work.

The ingredients and the basics of the process can easily be printed on a single page, and here's the good news: the average batch of homebrewed beer only takes a couple of hours from setup to cleanup (plus some time waiting around for that yeast to do its thing). Just let it ferment somewhere cool and dark for a few weeks, test it regularly, bottle it, and then decide if you're patient enough to let your new beer condition or mature in cold storage for another month or if you'd rather enjoy it sooner than that.

By now you might have already progressed beyond the most basic homebrewing concepts and techniques. Congratulations—you're probably ready for a new challenge. If you're new to the hobby, though, read on. This journal will be just as useful for you. One simple way to improve your skill as a homebrewer is to keep careful records and detailed notes of every batch you produce. Going back over these notes as you enjoy the fruits of your labor will help you better understand the process, identify problems and areas for improvement, and replicate your successes. In time, and as you slowly fill your journal with observations, dates, and measurements, you may discover an aptitude for experimenting or even designing your own recipes. Practice makes perfect, but perfection is often achieved more quickly when you remember what you did right. And when you do inevitably make some small mistake or miscalculation, follow Mr. Papazian's famously reassuring advice: relax, don't worry, and have a homebrew.

If you've already got wort bubbling away in a kettle on the stovetop and remain confident that everything is more or less under control, feel free to skip ahead to the recipe template and begin recording the specifics of your next beer-to-be. For a very quick refresher on the steps that happily lead from grain to glass, keep reading.

When beer is reduced down to its essential ingredients, this potentially complex, perpetually fascinating beverage becomes a lot less intimidating to the first-time brewer. Technically speaking, hops aren't entirely necessary to making beer (Google the word *gruit* to learn about ancestral ales), but to the modern beer enthusiast, this drink consists of malted (sprouted and dried) grain—most often barley and wheat—as well as hops, yeast, and water, a component that makes up about 90 percent of the final product. Plenty of other things can and do wind up in beer, especially in the creative, sophisticated age of brewing we currently live in, but these are the essential elements.

If you're brewing an extract beer to begin with, the steps to follow are short and sweet. Start by combining and dissolving your dry or liquid malt extract in the amount of water indicated in the recipe you're following, and bring it to a boil. Add any hops and/or brewing spices. Next, quickly chill the hot wort or unfermented beer you've just created in an ice bath and pitch the yeast. Transfer this liquid to a cleaned and sanitized (this is important) fermentation vessel, pouring in more water to reach the desired volume. Now you'll let the yeast, a single-celled organism, transform sugar into flavor, bubbles, and the fun stuff, alcohol.

If you've graduated to partial mash or all-grain recipes, there are a few more steps to pay attention to, but the outcome is the same: delicious beer. In this case you'll mash the milled and malted grain in boiling water before sparging (rinsing) it with hot water to pull out as much sugar as possible and then straining out the husks. Next you'll bring this wort to a second boil, adding hops as whole leaves, pellets, or plugs to impart bitterness, flavor, and aroma. After about an hour, you'll cool it down to approximately 70 degrees Fahrenheit so you don't kill the yeast you're about to add to finish the job. You didn't forget to sanitize your equipment first, did you? Finally, just like the extract method, you'll pitch your hungry fungi into the chilled wort, aerate it, and let the fermentation begin. Now, assuming you're able to keep your fermenting beer cool and out of direct sunlight, it will be ready to bottle or keg and drink soon enough.

In the pages that follow, you'll find a detailed homebrew template that should help you step up your homebrew skills over the course of a year. And by keeping track of the process, you'll find your beer steadily improving batch by batch. Plus, the handful of useful equations, glossary of common beer terms, and short list of further reading and online supply shops included at the back should make things that much easier.

BEER INFO

Beer Name: ____________________

____

Style: ____________________

Brewer(s): ____________________

____

❑ Partial Mash/Extract ❑ All-Grain

Preliminary Notes and Expectations

Gallons: ____________________

OG/FG: ____________________

ABV: ____________________

IBU: ____________________

SRM: ____________________

BREWING DAY

Date: ____________________

Start Time: ____________________

Beer(s) Imbibed: ____________________

____

____

____

____

____

Soundtrack: ____________________

____

____

____

____

____

INGREDIENTS

Grain Bill & Fermentables

	Amount	Cost
1.		
2.		
3.		
4.		
5.		
6.		
7.		
8.		

Hop Bill

	Amount	AA%	Cost
1.			
2.			
3.			
4.			
5.			
6.			

Other Ingredients

	Amount	Cost
1.		
2.		
3.		

Yeast

Variety: ____________________ Cost: ________

Water Adjustments

Notes: ____________________

Total Cost: ________

BREWING

STEP 1: Mash

❑ Single-Infusion ❑ Step-Infusion ❑ Decoction

Strike Water Amount: __________ Strike Water Temp: __________°

Starting Mash Temp: __________° Final Mash Temp: __________°

Sparge Water Amount: __________ Sparge Water Temp: __________°

Sparge Temp: __________°

Pre-boil Gravity: __________

Notes: ______________________________

____

For Extract Batches

Water Volume: __________

Grains Steeped for: __________ minutes at __________°

Extract(s) Added: ❑ Start of Boil ❑ __________ Minutes into Boil

STEP 2: Boil

Hops & Other Ingredients Schedule

		Time
1.	______________________________	__________
2.	______________________________	__________
3.	______________________________	__________
4.	______________________________	__________
5.	______________________________	__________
6.	______________________________	__________

STEP 3: Chilling and Pitching

Chill Method: ❑ Ice Bath ❑ Immersion Coil ❑ __________

Chill Start Time: __________

Chill Finish Time: __________

Original Gravity: __________

Wort Temp at Pitching: __________°

Wort Volume: __________

Aeration Method: ❑ Agitation ❑ Forced

Notes: ______________________________

FERMENTATION

Primary Start Date/Time: ______

❑ Glass Carboy ❑ Plastic Bucket ❑ ______

❑ Airlock ❑ Blow-off Tube ❑ ______

Date/Time: ______ Temp: ______°

Date/Time: ______ Temp: ______°

Date/Time: ______ Temp: ______°

Date/Time: ______ Temp: ______°

Date/Time: ______ Temp: ______°

Date/Time: ______ Temp: ______°

Date/Time: ______ Temp: ______°

Date/Time: ______ Temp: ______°

Additions to Primary or Secondary: ______

Secondary Start Date/Time: ______

Date/Time: ______ Temp: ______°

Date/Time: ______ Temp: ______°

Date/Time: ______ Temp: ______°

Date/Time: ______ Temp: ______°

Date/Time: ______ Temp: ______°

Date/Time: ______ Temp: ______°

Date/Time: ______ Temp: ______°

Date/Time: ______ Temp: ______°

Notes: ______

PACKAGING

Date/Time: ______

Final Gravity: ______

(____ OG – ____ FG) × 131 = ____% ABV

❑ Bottle ❑ Keg

Priming Agent: ______

Amount: ______

-or-

CO_2 Setting: ______ psi for ____ days

Sanitizing Agent/Method: ______

STORAGE/AGING

Date/Time: ______ Temp: ______°

Date/Time: ______ Temp: ______°

Date/Time: ______ Temp: ______°

Date/Time: ______ Temp: ______°

Date/Time: ______ Temp: ______°

Date/Time: ______ Temp: ______°

Notes: ______

FIRST TASTING

Date/Time: ____________________

Tasters: ____________________

Glassware: ____________________

Serving Temp: __________°

Appearance: ____________________

Aroma: ____________________

Flavor: ____________________

Finish: ____________________

FINAL THOUGHTS

BEER INFO

Beer Name: ______________________

____

Style: ______________________

Brewer(s): ______________________

____

❑ Partial Mash/Extract ❑ All-Grain

Preliminary Notes and Expectations

Gallons: ______________________

OG/FG: ______________________

ABV: ______________________

IBU: ______________________

SRM: ______________________

BREWING DAY

Date: ______________________

Start Time: ______________________

Beer(s) Imbibed: ______________________

____

____

____

____

____

Soundtrack: ______________________

____

____

____

____

____

INGREDIENTS

Grain Bill & Fermentables

	Amount	Cost
1.		
2.		
3.		
4.		
5.		
6.		
7.		
8.		

Hop Bill

	Amount	AA%	Cost
1.			
2.			
3.			
4.			
5.			
6.			

Other Ingredients

	Amount	Cost
1.		
2.		
3.		

Yeast

Variety: ______________________ Cost: __________

Water Adjustments

Notes: ______________________

Total Cost: __________

BREWING

Step 1: Mash

❑ Single-Infusion ❑ Step-Infusion ❑ Decoction

Strike Water Amount: __________ Strike Water Temp: __________°

Starting Mash Temp: __________° Final Mash Temp: __________°

Sparge Water Amount: __________ Sparge Water Temp: __________°

Sparge Temp: __________°

Pre-boil Gravity: __________

Notes: ______________________________

____

For Extract Batches

Water Volume: __________

Grains Steeped for: __________ minutes at __________°

Extract(s) Added: ❑ Start of Boil ❑ __________ Minutes into Boil

Step 2: Boil

Hops & Other Ingredients Schedule

	Time
1. ______________________________	__________
2. ______________________________	__________
3. ______________________________	__________
4. ______________________________	__________
5. ______________________________	__________
6. ______________________________	__________

Step 3: Chilling and Pitching

Chill Method: ❑ Ice Bath ❑ Immersion Coil ❑ __________

Chill Start Time: __________

Chill Finish Time: __________

Original Gravity: __________

Wort Temp at Pitching: __________°

Wort Volume: __________

Aeration Method: ❑ Agitation ❑ Forced

Notes: ______________________________

FERMENTATION

Primary Start Date/Time: ____________________

❑ Glass Carboy ❑ Plastic Bucket ❑ ____________

❑ Airlock ❑ Blow-off Tube ❑ ____________

Date/Time: ____________________ Temp: ______°

Date/Time: ____________________ Temp: ______°

Date/Time: ____________________ Temp: ______°

Date/Time: ____________________ Temp: ______°

Date/Time: ____________________ Temp: ______°

Date/Time: ____________________ Temp: ______°

Date/Time: ____________________ Temp: ______°

Date/Time: ____________________ Temp: ______°

Additions to Primary or Secondary: ____________________

Secondary Start Date/Time: ____________________

Date/Time: ____________________ Temp: ______°

Date/Time: ____________________ Temp: ______°

Date/Time: ____________________ Temp: ______°

Date/Time: ____________________ Temp: ______°

Date/Time: ____________________ Temp: ______°

Date/Time: ____________________ Temp: ______°

Date/Time: ____________________ Temp: ______°

Date/Time: ____________________ Temp: ______°

Notes: ____________________

PACKAGING

Date/Time: ____________________

Final Gravity: ____________________

(______ OG – ______ FG) × 131 = ______% ABV

❑ Bottle ❑ Keg

Priming Agent: ____________________

Amount: ____________________

-or-

CO_2 Setting: ________ psi for ______ days

Sanitizing Agent/Method: ____________________

STORAGE/AGING

Date/Time: __________ Temp: ______°

Date/Time: __________ Temp: ______°

Date/Time: __________ Temp: ______°

Date/Time: __________ Temp: ______°

Date/Time: __________ Temp: ______°

Date/Time: __________ Temp: ______°

Notes: ____________________

FIRST TASTING

Date/Time: ______________________

Tasters: ______________________

Glassware: ______________________

Serving Temp: __________°

Appearance: ______________________

Aroma: ______________________

Flavor: ______________________

Finish: ______________________

FINAL THOUGHTS

BEER INFO

Beer Name: ____________________

____

Style: ____________________

Brewer(s): ____________________

____

❑ Partial Mash/Extract ❑ All-Grain

Preliminary Notes and Expectations

Gallons: ____________________

OG/FG: ____________________

ABV: ____________________

IBU: ____________________

SRM: ____________________

BREWING DAY

Date: ____________________

Start Time: ____________________

Beer(s) Imbibed: ____________________

____

____

____

____

____

Soundtrack: ____________________

____

____

____

____

____

INGREDIENTS

Grain Bill & Fermentables

	Amount	Cost
1.		
2.		
3.		
4.		
5.		
6.		
7.		
8.		

Hop Bill

	Amount	AA%	Cost
1.			
2.			
3.			
4.			
5.			
6.			

Other Ingredients

	Amount	Cost
1.		
2.		
3.		

Yeast

Variety: ____________________ Cost: __________

Water Adjustments

Notes: ____________________

Total Cost: __________

BREWING

Step 1: Mash

❑ Single-Infusion ❑ Step-Infusion ❑ Decoction

Strike Water Amount: __________ Strike Water Temp: __________°

Starting Mash Temp: __________° Final Mash Temp: __________°

Sparge Water Amount: __________ Sparge Water Temp: __________°

Sparge Temp: __________°

Pre-boil Gravity: __________

Notes: ____

____

For Extract Batches

Water Volume: __________

Grains Steeped for: __________ minutes at __________°

Extract(s) Added: ❑ Start of Boil ❑ __________ Minutes into Boil

Step 2: Boil

Hops & Other Ingredients Schedule

	Time
1. ____________________	__________
2. ____________________	__________
3. ____________________	__________
4. ____________________	__________
5. ____________________	__________
6. ____________________	__________

Step 3: Chilling and Pitching

Chill Method: ❑ Ice Bath ❑ Immersion Coil ❑ __________

Chill Start Time: __________

Chill Finish Time: __________

Original Gravity: __________

Wort Temp at Pitching: __________°

Wort Volume: __________

Aeration Method: ❑ Agitation ❑ Forced

Notes: ____

FERMENTATION

Primary Start Date/Time: ______

❑ Glass Carboy ❑ Plastic Bucket ❑ ______

❑ Airlock ❑ Blow-off Tube ❑ ______

Date/Time: ______ Temp: ______°

Date/Time: ______ Temp: ______°

Date/Time: ______ Temp: ______°

Date/Time: ______ Temp: ______°

Date/Time: ______ Temp: ______°

Date/Time: ______ Temp: ______°

Date/Time: ______ Temp: ______°

Date/Time: ______ Temp: ______°

Additions to Primary or Secondary: ______

Secondary Start Date/Time: ______

Date/Time: ______ Temp: ______°

Date/Time: ______ Temp: ______°

Date/Time: ______ Temp: ______°

Date/Time: ______ Temp: ______°

Date/Time: ______ Temp: ______°

Date/Time: ______ Temp: ______°

Date/Time: ______ Temp: ______°

Date/Time: ______ Temp: ______°

Notes: ______

PACKAGING

Date/Time: ______

Final Gravity: ______

(______ OG – ______ FG) × 131 = ______% ABV

❑ Bottle ❑ Keg

Priming Agent: ______

Amount: ______

-or-

CO_2 Setting: ______ psi for ______ days

Sanitizing Agent/Method: ______

STORAGE/AGING

Date/Time: ______ Temp: ______°

Date/Time: ______ Temp: ______°

Date/Time: ______ Temp: ______°

Date/Time: ______ Temp: ______°

Date/Time: ______ Temp: ______°

Date/Time: ______ Temp: ______°

Notes: ______

FIRST TASTING

Date/Time: ___

Tasters: ___

Glassware: ___

Serving Temp: ___°

Appearance: ___

Aroma: ___

Flavor: ___

Finish: ___

FINAL THOUGHTS

BEER INFO

Beer Name: ____________________

____

Style: ____________________

Brewer(s): ____________________

____

❑ Partial Mash/Extract ❑ All-Grain

Preliminary Notes and Expectations

Gallons: ____________________

OG/FG: ____________________

ABV: ____________________

IBU: ____________________

SRM: ____________________

BREWING DAY

Date: ____________________

Start Time: ____________________

Beer(s) Imbibed: ____________________

____

____

____

____

____

Soundtrack: ____________________

____

____

____

____

____

INGREDIENTS

Grain Bill & Fermentables

	Amount	Cost
1. ____________	______	______
2. ____________	______	______
3. ____________	______	______
4. ____________	______	______
5. ____________	______	______
6. ____________	______	______
7. ____________	______	______
8. ____________	______	______

Hop Bill

	Amount	AA%	Cost
1. ____________	______	______	______
2. ____________	______	______	______
3. ____________	______	______	______
4. ____________	______	______	______
5. ____________	______	______	______
6. ____________	______	______	______

Other Ingredients

	Amount	Cost
1. ____________	______	______
2. ____________	______	______
3. ____________	______	______

Yeast

Variety: ____________________ Cost: ________

Water Adjustments

Notes: ____________________

Total Cost: ________

BREWING

Step 1: Mash

❑ Single-Infusion ❑ Step-Infusion ❑ Decoction

Strike Water Amount: ________ Strike Water Temp: ________°

Starting Mash Temp: ________° Final Mash Temp: ________°

Sparge Water Amount: ________ Sparge Water Temp: ________°

Sparge Temp: ________°

Pre-boil Gravity: ________

Notes: ____

____

For Extract Batches

Water Volume: ________

Grains Steeped for: ________ minutes at ________°

Extract(s) Added: ❑ Start of Boil ❑ ________ Minutes into Boil

Step 2: Boil

Hops & Other Ingredients Schedule

	Time
1. ________________________________	________
2. ________________________________	________
3. ________________________________	________
4. ________________________________	________
5. ________________________________	________
6. ________________________________	________

Step 3: Chilling and Pitching

Chill Method: ❑ Ice Bath ❑ Immersion Coil ❑ ________

Chill Start Time: ________

Chill Finish Time: ________

Original Gravity: ________

Wort Temp at Pitching: ________°

Wort Volume: ________

Aeration Method: ❑ Agitation ❑ Forced

Notes: ________________________________

FERMENTATION

Primary Start Date/Time: ____________________

❑ Glass Carboy ❑ Plastic Bucket ❑ __________

❑ Airlock ❑ Blow-off Tube ❑ __________

Date/Time: ____________________ Temp: ______°

Date/Time: ____________________ Temp: ______°

Date/Time: ____________________ Temp: ______°

Date/Time: ____________________ Temp: ______°

Date/Time: ____________________ Temp: ______°

Date/Time: ____________________ Temp: ______°

Date/Time: ____________________ Temp: ______°

Date/Time: ____________________ Temp: ______°

Additions to Primary or Secondary: ____________________

Secondary Start Date/Time: ____________________

Date/Time: ____________________ Temp: ______°

Date/Time: ____________________ Temp: ______°

Date/Time: ____________________ Temp: ______°

Date/Time: ____________________ Temp: ______°

Date/Time: ____________________ Temp: ______°

Date/Time: ____________________ Temp: ______°

Date/Time: ____________________ Temp: ______°

Date/Time: ____________________ Temp: ______°

Notes: ____________________

PACKAGING

Date/Time: ____________________

Final Gravity: ____________________

(_____ OG – _____ FG) × 131 = _____% ABV

❑ Bottle ❑ Keg

Priming Agent: ____________________

Amount: ____________________

-or-

CO_2 Setting: __________ psi for _____ days

Sanitizing Agent/Method: ____________________

STORAGE/AGING

Date/Time: __________ Temp: ______°

Date/Time: __________ Temp: ______°

Date/Time: __________ Temp: ______°

Date/Time: __________ Temp: ______°

Date/Time: __________ Temp: ______°

Date/Time: __________ Temp: ______°

Notes: ____________________

FIRST TASTING

Date/Time: __________

Tasters: __________

Glassware: __________

Serving Temp: __________ °

Appearance: __________

Aroma: __________

Flavor: __________

Finish: __________

FINAL THOUGHTS

BEER INFO

Beer Name: ______________________

____

Style: ______________________

Brewer(s): ______________________

____

❑ Partial Mash/Extract ❑ All-Grain

Preliminary Notes and Expectations

Gallons: ______________________

OG/FG: ______________________

ABV: ______________________

IBU: ______________________

SRM: ______________________

BREWING DAY

Date: ______________________

Start Time: ______________________

Beer(s) Imbibed: ______________________

____

____

____

____

____

Soundtrack: ______________________

____

____

____

____

____

INGREDIENTS

Grain Bill & Fermentables

	Amount	Cost
1.		
2.		
3.		
4.		
5.		
6.		
7.		
8.		

Hop Bill

	Amount	AA%	Cost
1.			
2.			
3.			
4.			
5.			
6.			

Other Ingredients

	Amount	Cost
1.		
2.		
3.		

Yeast

Variety: ______________________ Cost: ________

Water Adjustments

Notes: ______________________

Total Cost: ________

BREWING

STEP 1: Mash

❑ Single-Infusion ❑ Step-Infusion ❑ Decoction

Strike Water Amount: ________ Strike Water Temp: ________°

Starting Mash Temp: ________° Final Mash Temp: ________°

Sparge Water Amount: ________ Sparge Water Temp: ________°

Sparge Temp: ________°

Pre-boil Gravity: ________

Notes: ____

____

For Extract Batches

Water Volume: ________

Grains Steeped for: ________ minutes at ________°

Extract(s) Added: ❑ Start of Boil ❑ ________ Minutes into Boil

STEP 2: Boil

Hops & Other Ingredients Schedule

	Time
1. ________________________________	________
2. ________________________________	________
3. ________________________________	________
4. ________________________________	________
5. ________________________________	________
6. ________________________________	________

STEP 3: Chilling and Pitching

Chill Method: ❑ Ice Bath ❑ Immersion Coil ❑ ________

Chill Start Time: ________

Chill Finish Time: ________

Original Gravity: ________

Wort Temp at Pitching: ________°

Wort Volume: ________

Aeration Method: ❑ Agitation ❑ Forced

Notes: ________________________________

FERMENTATION

Primary Start Date/Time: ____

❑ Glass Carboy ❑ Plastic Bucket ❑ ____

❑ Airlock ❑ Blow-off Tube ❑ ____

Date/Time: ____ Temp: ____°

Date/Time: ____ Temp: ____°

Date/Time: ____ Temp: ____°

Date/Time: ____ Temp: ____°

Date/Time: ____ Temp: ____°

Date/Time: ____ Temp: ____°

Date/Time: ____ Temp: ____°

Date/Time: ____ Temp: ____°

Additions to Primary or Secondary: ____

Secondary Start Date/Time: ____

Date/Time: ____ Temp: ____°

Date/Time: ____ Temp: ____°

Date/Time: ____ Temp: ____°

Date/Time: ____ Temp: ____°

Date/Time: ____ Temp: ____°

Date/Time: ____ Temp: ____°

Date/Time: ____ Temp: ____°

Date/Time: ____ Temp: ____°

Notes: ____

PACKAGING

Date/Time: ____

Final Gravity: ____

(____ OG – ____ FG) × 131 = ____% ABV

❑ Bottle ❑ Keg

Priming Agent: ____

Amount: ____

-or-

CO_2 Setting: ____ psi for ____ days

Sanitizing Agent/Method: ____

STORAGE/AGING

Date/Time: ____ Temp: ____°

Date/Time: ____ Temp: ____°

Date/Time: ____ Temp: ____°

Date/Time: ____ Temp: ____°

Date/Time: ____ Temp: ____°

Date/Time: ____ Temp: ____°

Notes: ____

FIRST TASTING

Date/Time:

Tasters:

Glassware:

Serving Temp: °

Appearance:

Aroma:

Flavor:

Finish:

FINAL THOUGHTS

BEER INFO

Beer Name: ______________________

____

Style: ______________________

Brewer(s): ______________________

____

❑ Partial Mash/Extract ❑ All-Grain

Preliminary Notes and Expectations

Gallons: ______________________

OG/FG: ______________________

ABV: ______________________

IBU: ______________________

SRM: ______________________

BREWING DAY

Date: ______________________

Start Time: ______________________

Beer(s) Imbibed: ______________________

____

____

____

____

____

Soundtrack: ______________________

____

____

____

____

____

INGREDIENTS

Grain Bill & Fermentables

	Amount	Cost
1.		
2.		
3.		
4.		
5.		
6.		
7.		
8.		

Hop Bill

	Amount	AA%	Cost
1.			
2.			
3.			
4.			
5.			
6.			

Other Ingredients

	Amount	Cost
1.		
2.		
3.		

Yeast

Variety: ______________________ Cost: __________

Water Adjustments

Notes: ______________________

Total Cost: __________

BREWING

Step 1: Mash

❑ Single-Infusion ❑ Step-Infusion ❑ Decoction

Strike Water Amount: ________ Strike Water Temp: ________°

Starting Mash Temp: ________° Final Mash Temp: ________°

Sparge Water Amount: ________ Sparge Water Temp: ________°

Sparge Temp: ________°

Pre-boil Gravity: ________

Notes: ________

____

For Extract Batches

Water Volume: ________

Grains Steeped for: ________ minutes at ________°

Extract(s) Added: ❑ Start of Boil ❑ ________ Minutes into Boil

Step 2: Boil

Hops & Other Ingredients Schedule

	Time
1. ________	________
2. ________	________
3. ________	________
4. ________	________
5. ________	________
6. ________	________

Step 3: Chilling and Pitching

Chill Method: ❑ Ice Bath ❑ Immersion Coil ❑ ________

Chill Start Time: ________

Chill Finish Time: ________

Original Gravity: ________

Wort Temp at Pitching: ________°

Wort Volume: ________

Aeration Method: ❑ Agitation ❑ Forced

Notes: ________

FERMENTATION

Primary Start Date/Time: ______________________

❑ Glass Carboy ❑ Plastic Bucket ❑ ____________

❑ Airlock ❑ Blow-off Tube ❑ ____________

Date/Time: ______________________ Temp: ________°

Date/Time: ______________________ Temp: ________°

Date/Time: ______________________ Temp: ________°

Date/Time: ______________________ Temp: ________°

Date/Time: ______________________ Temp: ________°

Date/Time: ______________________ Temp: ________°

Date/Time: ______________________ Temp: ________°

Date/Time: ______________________ Temp: ________°

Additions to Primary or Secondary: ______________________

____

____

____

____

Secondary Start Date/Time: ______________________

Date/Time: ______________________ Temp: ________°

Date/Time: ______________________ Temp: ________°

Date/Time: ______________________ Temp: ________°

Date/Time: ______________________ Temp: ________°

Date/Time: ______________________ Temp: ________°

Date/Time: ______________________ Temp: ________°

Date/Time: ______________________ Temp: ________°

Date/Time: ______________________ Temp: ________°

Notes: ______________________

____

____

____

____

PACKAGING

Date/Time: ______________________

Final Gravity: ______________________

(_____ OG – _____ FG) × 131 = _____% ABV

❑ Bottle ❑ Keg

Priming Agent: ______________________

Amount: ______________________

-or-

CO_2 Setting: ________ psi for _____ days

Sanitizing Agent/Method: ______________________

____

____

STORAGE/AGING

Date/Time: __________ Temp: ________°

Date/Time: __________ Temp: ________°

Date/Time: __________ Temp: ________°

Date/Time: __________ Temp: ________°

Date/Time: __________ Temp: ________°

Date/Time: __________ Temp: ________°

Notes: ______________________

____

____

____

____

____

____

____

____

____

FIRST TASTING

Date/Time: ______________________

Tasters: ______________________

Glassware: ______________________

Serving Temp: __________°

Appearance: ______________________

Aroma: ______________________

Flavor: ______________________

Finish: ______________________

FINAL THOUGHTS

BEER INFO

Beer Name: ______________________

____

Style: ______________________

Brewer(s): ______________________

____

❑ Partial Mash/Extract ❑ All-Grain

Preliminary Notes and Expectations

Gallons: ______________________

OG/FG: ______________________

ABV: ______________________

IBU: ______________________

SRM: ______________________

BREWING DAY

Date: ______________________

Start Time: ______________________

Beer(s) Imbibed: ______________________

____

____

____

____

____

Soundtrack: ______________________

____

____

____

____

____

INGREDIENTS

Grain Bill & Fermentables

	Amount	Cost
1.		
2.		
3.		
4.		
5.		
6.		
7.		
8.		

Hop Bill

	Amount	AA%	Cost
1.			
2.			
3.			
4.			
5.			
6.			

Other Ingredients

	Amount	Cost
1.		
2.		
3.		

Yeast

Variety: ______________________ Cost: __________

Water Adjustments

Notes: ______________________

Total Cost: __________

BREWING

Step 1: Mash

❑ Single-Infusion ❑ Step-Infusion ❑ Decoction

Strike Water Amount: __________ Strike Water Temp: __________°

Starting Mash Temp: __________° Final Mash Temp: __________°

Sparge Water Amount: __________ Sparge Water Temp: __________°

Sparge Temp: __________°

Pre-boil Gravity: __________

Notes: ______________________________

____

For Extract Batches

Water Volume: __________

Grains Steeped for: __________ minutes at __________°

Extract(s) Added: ❑ Start of Boil ❑ __________ Minutes into Boil

Step 2: Boil

Hops & Other Ingredients Schedule

	Time
1. ______________________________	__________
2. ______________________________	__________
3. ______________________________	__________
4. ______________________________	__________
5. ______________________________	__________
6. ______________________________	__________

Step 3: Chilling and Pitching

Chill Method: ❑ Ice Bath ❑ Immersion Coil ❑ __________

Chill Start Time: __________

Chill Finish Time: __________

Original Gravity: __________

Wort Temp at Pitching: __________°

Wort Volume: __________

Aeration Method: ❑ Agitation ❑ Forced

Notes: ______________________________

FERMENTATION

Primary Start Date/Time: ______

❑ Glass Carboy ❑ Plastic Bucket ❑ ______

❑ Airlock ❑ Blow-off Tube ❑ ______

Date/Time: ______ Temp: ______°

Date/Time: ______ Temp: ______°

Date/Time: ______ Temp: ______°

Date/Time: ______ Temp: ______°

Date/Time: ______ Temp: ______°

Date/Time: ______ Temp: ______°

Date/Time: ______ Temp: ______°

Date/Time: ______ Temp: ______°

Additions to Primary or Secondary: ______

Secondary Start Date/Time: ______

Date/Time: ______ Temp: ______°

Date/Time: ______ Temp: ______°

Date/Time: ______ Temp: ______°

Date/Time: ______ Temp: ______°

Date/Time: ______ Temp: ______°

Date/Time: ______ Temp: ______°

Date/Time: ______ Temp: ______°

Date/Time: ______ Temp: ______°

Notes: ______

PACKAGING

Date/Time: ______

Final Gravity: ______

(______ OG – ______ FG) × 131 = ______% ABV

❑ Bottle ❑ Keg

Priming Agent: ______

Amount: ______

-or-

CO_2 Setting: ______ psi for ______ days

Sanitizing Agent/Method: ______

STORAGE/AGING

Date/Time: ______ Temp: ______°

Date/Time: ______ Temp: ______°

Date/Time: ______ Temp: ______°

Date/Time: ______ Temp: ______°

Date/Time: ______ Temp: ______°

Date/Time: ______ Temp: ______°

Notes: ______

FIRST TASTING

Date/Time: ______

Tasters: ______

Glassware: ______

Serving Temp: ______°

Appearance: ______

Aroma: ______

Flavor: ______

Finish: ______

FINAL THOUGHTS

BEER INFO

Beer Name: ____________________

____

Style: ____________________

Brewer(s): ____________________

____

❑ Partial Mash/Extract ❑ All-Grain

Preliminary Notes and Expectations

Gallons: ____________________

OG/FG: ____________________

ABV: ____________________

IBU: ____________________

SRM: ____________________

BREWING DAY

Date: ____________________

Start Time: ____________________

Beer(s) Imbibed: ____________________

____

____

____

____

____

Soundtrack: ____________________

____

____

____

____

____

INGREDIENTS

Grain Bill & Fermentables

	Amount	Cost
1.		
2.		
3.		
4.		
5.		
6.		
7.		
8.		

Hop Bill

	Amount	AA%	Cost
1.			
2.			
3.			
4.			
5.			
6.			

Other Ingredients

	Amount	Cost
1.		
2.		
3.		

Yeast

Variety: ____________________ Cost: ________

Water Adjustments

Notes: ____________________

Total Cost: ________

BREWING

Step 1: Mash

❑ Single-Infusion ❑ Step-Infusion ❑ Decoction

Strike Water Amount: ________ Strike Water Temp: ________°

Starting Mash Temp: ________° Final Mash Temp: ________°

Sparge Water Amount: ________ Sparge Water Temp: ________°

Sparge Temp: ________°

Pre-boil Gravity: ________

Notes: ____

____

For Extract Batches

Water Volume: ________

Grains Steeped for: ________ minutes at ________°

Extract(s) Added: ❑ Start of Boil ❑ ________ Minutes into Boil

Step 2: Boil

Hops & Other Ingredients Schedule

		Time
1.	________________________________	________
2.	________________________________	________
3.	________________________________	________
4.	________________________________	________
5.	________________________________	________
6.	________________________________	________

Step 3: Chilling and Pitching

Chill Method: ❑ Ice Bath ❑ Immersion Coil ❑ ________

Chill Start Time: ________

Chill Finish Time: ________

Original Gravity: ________

Wort Temp at Pitching: ________°

Wort Volume: ________

Aeration Method: ❑ Agitation ❑ Forced

Notes: ________________________________

FERMENTATION

Primary Start Date/Time: ______

❑ Glass Carboy ❑ Plastic Bucket ❑ ______

❑ Airlock ❑ Blow-off Tube ❑ ______

Date/Time: ______ Temp: ______°

Date/Time: ______ Temp: ______°

Date/Time: ______ Temp: ______°

Date/Time: ______ Temp: ______°

Date/Time: ______ Temp: ______°

Date/Time: ______ Temp: ______°

Date/Time: ______ Temp: ______°

Date/Time: ______ Temp: ______°

Additions to Primary or Secondary: ______

______

______

______

______

Secondary Start Date/Time: ______

Date/Time: ______ Temp: ______°

Date/Time: ______ Temp: ______°

Date/Time: ______ Temp: ______°

Date/Time: ______ Temp: ______°

Date/Time: ______ Temp: ______°

Date/Time: ______ Temp: ______°

Date/Time: ______ Temp: ______°

Date/Time: ______ Temp: ______°

Notes: ______

______

______

______

______

PACKAGING

Date/Time: ______

Final Gravity: ______

(______ OG – ______ FG) × 131 = ______% ABV

❑ Bottle ❑ Keg

Priming Agent: ______

Amount: ______

-or-

CO_2 Setting: ______ psi for ______ days

Sanitizing Agent/Method: ______

______

______

STORAGE/AGING

Date/Time: ______ Temp: ______°

Date/Time: ______ Temp: ______°

Date/Time: ______ Temp: ______°

Date/Time: ______ Temp: ______°

Date/Time: ______ Temp: ______°

Date/Time: ______ Temp: ______°

Notes: ______

______

______

______

______

______

______

______

______

______

FIRST TASTING

Date/Time: ______

Tasters: ______

Glassware: ______

Serving Temp: ______°

Appearance: ______

Aroma: ______

Flavor: ______

Finish: ______

FINAL THOUGHTS

BEER INFO

Beer Name: ______________________

____

Style: ______________________

Brewer(s): ______________________

____

❑ Partial Mash/Extract ❑ All-Grain

Preliminary Notes and Expectations

Gallons: ______________________

OG/FG: ______________________

ABV: ______________________

IBU: ______________________

SRM: ______________________

BREWING DAY

Date: ______________________

Start Time: ______________________

Beer(s) Imbibed: ______________________

____

____

____

____

____

Soundtrack: ______________________

____

____

____

____

____

INGREDIENTS

Grain Bill & Fermentables

	Amount	Cost
1.		
2.		
3.		
4.		
5.		
6.		
7.		
8.		

Hop Bill

	Amount	AA%	Cost
1.			
2.			
3.			
4.			
5.			
6.			

Other Ingredients

	Amount	Cost
1.		
2.		
3.		

Yeast

Variety: ______________________ Cost: __________

Water Adjustments

Notes: ______________________

Total Cost: __________

BREWING

Step 1: Mash

❑ Single-Infusion ❑ Step-Infusion ❑ Decoction

Strike Water Amount: __________ Strike Water Temp: __________°

Starting Mash Temp: __________° Final Mash Temp: __________°

Sparge Water Amount: __________ Sparge Water Temp: __________°

Sparge Temp: __________°

Pre-boil Gravity: __________

Notes: ____

____

For Extract Batches

Water Volume: __________

Grains Steeped for: __________ minutes at __________°

Extract(s) Added: ❑ Start of Boil ❑ __________ Minutes into Boil

Step 2: Boil

Hops & Other Ingredients Schedule

		Time
1.	______________________________	__________
2.	______________________________	__________
3.	______________________________	__________
4.	______________________________	__________
5.	______________________________	__________
6.	______________________________	__________

Step 3: Chilling and Pitching

Chill Method: ❑ Ice Bath ❑ Immersion Coil ❑ __________

Chill Start Time: __________

Chill Finish Time: __________

Original Gravity: __________

Wort Temp at Pitching: __________°

Wort Volume: __________

Aeration Method: ❑ Agitation ❑ Forced

Notes: ____

FERMENTATION

Primary Start Date/Time: ______

❑ Glass Carboy ❑ Plastic Bucket ❑ ______

❑ Airlock ❑ Blow-off Tube ❑ ______

Date/Time: ______ Temp: ______°

Date/Time: ______ Temp: ______°

Date/Time: ______ Temp: ______°

Date/Time: ______ Temp: ______°

Date/Time: ______ Temp: ______°

Date/Time: ______ Temp: ______°

Date/Time: ______ Temp: ______°

Date/Time: ______ Temp: ______°

Additions to Primary or Secondary: ______

Secondary Start Date/Time: ______

Date/Time: ______ Temp: ______°

Date/Time: ______ Temp: ______°

Date/Time: ______ Temp: ______°

Date/Time: ______ Temp: ______°

Date/Time: ______ Temp: ______°

Date/Time: ______ Temp: ______°

Date/Time: ______ Temp: ______°

Date/Time: ______ Temp: ______°

Notes: ______

PACKAGING

Date/Time: ______

Final Gravity: ______

(____ OG – ____ FG) × 131 = ____% ABV

❑ Bottle ❑ Keg

Priming Agent: ______

Amount: ______

-or-

CO_2 Setting: ______ psi for ____ days

Sanitizing Agent/Method: ______

STORAGE/AGING

Date/Time: ______ Temp: ______°

Date/Time: ______ Temp: ______°

Date/Time: ______ Temp: ______°

Date/Time: ______ Temp: ______°

Date/Time: ______ Temp: ______°

Date/Time: ______ Temp: ______°

Notes: ______

FIRST TASTING

Date/Time: ______

Tasters: ______

Glassware: ______

Serving Temp: ______°

Appearance: ______

Aroma: ______

Flavor: ______

Finish: ______

FINAL THOUGHTS

BEER INFO

Beer Name: ____________________

____

Style: ____________________

Brewer(s): ____________________

____

❑ Partial Mash/Extract ❑ All-Grain

Preliminary Notes and Expectations

Gallons: ____________________

OG/FG: ____________________

ABV: ____________________

IBU: ____________________

SRM: ____________________

BREWING DAY

Date: ____________________

Start Time: ____________________

Beer(s) Imbibed: ____________________

____

____

____

____

____

Soundtrack: ____________________

____

____

____

____

____

INGREDIENTS

Grain Bill & Fermentables

	Amount	Cost
1.		
2.		
3.		
4.		
5.		
6.		
7.		
8.		

Hop Bill

	Amount	AA%	Cost
1.			
2.			
3.			
4.			
5.			
6.			

Other Ingredients

	Amount	Cost
1.		
2.		
3.		

Yeast

Variety: ____________________ Cost: ________

Water Adjustments

Notes: ____________________

Total Cost: ________

BREWING

STEP 1: Mash

❑ Single-Infusion ❑ Step-Infusion ❑ Decoction

Strike Water Amount: ________ Strike Water Temp: ________°

Starting Mash Temp: ________° Final Mash Temp: ________°

Sparge Water Amount: ________ Sparge Water Temp: ________°

Sparge Temp: ________°

Pre-boil Gravity: ________

Notes: ____

____

For Extract Batches

Water Volume: ________

Grains Steeped for: ________ minutes at ________°

Extract(s) Added: ❑ Start of Boil ❑ ________ Minutes into Boil

STEP 2: Boil

Hops & Other Ingredients Schedule

		Time
1.	________________________	________
2.	________________________	________
3.	________________________	________
4.	________________________	________
5.	________________________	________
6.	________________________	________

STEP 3: Chilling and Pitching

Chill Method: ❑ Ice Bath ❑ Immersion Coil ❑ ________

Chill Start Time: ________

Chill Finish Time: ________

Original Gravity: ________

Wort Temp at Pitching: ________°

Wort Volume: ________

Aeration Method: ❑ Agitation ❑ Forced

Notes: ____

FERMENTATION

Primary Start Date/Time: ______

❑ Glass Carboy ❑ Plastic Bucket ❑ ______

❑ Airlock ❑ Blow-off Tube ❑ ______

Date/Time: ______ Temp: ______°

Date/Time: ______ Temp: ______°

Date/Time: ______ Temp: ______°

Date/Time: ______ Temp: ______°

Date/Time: ______ Temp: ______°

Date/Time: ______ Temp: ______°

Date/Time: ______ Temp: ______°

Date/Time: ______ Temp: ______°

Additions to Primary or Secondary: ______

Secondary Start Date/Time: ______

Date/Time: ______ Temp: ______°

Date/Time: ______ Temp: ______°

Date/Time: ______ Temp: ______°

Date/Time: ______ Temp: ______°

Date/Time: ______ Temp: ______°

Date/Time: ______ Temp: ______°

Date/Time: ______ Temp: ______°

Date/Time: ______ Temp: ______°

Notes: ______

PACKAGING

Date/Time: ______

Final Gravity: ______

(______ OG – ______ FG) × 131 = ______% ABV

❑ Bottle ❑ Keg

Priming Agent: ______

Amount: ______

-or-

CO_2 Setting: ______ psi for ______ days

Sanitizing Agent/Method: ______

STORAGE/AGING

Date/Time: ______ Temp: ______°

Date/Time: ______ Temp: ______°

Date/Time: ______ Temp: ______°

Date/Time: ______ Temp: ______°

Date/Time: ______ Temp: ______°

Date/Time: ______ Temp: ______°

Notes: ______

FIRST TASTING

Date/Time: ____________________

Tasters: ____________________

Glassware: ____________________

Serving Temp: __________°

Appearance: ____________________

Aroma: ____________________

Flavor: ____________________

Finish: ____________________

FINAL THOUGHTS

BEER INFO

Beer Name: ____________________

____

Style: ____________________

Brewer(s): ____________________

____

❏ Partial Mash/Extract ❏ All-Grain

Preliminary Notes and Expectations

Gallons: ____________________

OG/FG: ____________________

ABV: ____________________

IBU: ____________________

SRM: ____________________

BREWING DAY

Date: ____________________

Start Time: ____________________

Beer(s) Imbibed: ____________________

____

____

____

____

____

Soundtrack: ____________________

____

____

____

____

____

INGREDIENTS

Grain Bill & Fermentables

	Amount	Cost
1.		
2.		
3.		
4.		
5.		
6.		
7.		
8.		

Hop Bill

	Amount	AA%	Cost
1.			
2.			
3.			
4.			
5.			
6.			

Other Ingredients

	Amount	Cost
1.		
2.		
3.		

Yeast

Variety: ____________________ Cost: __________

Water Adjustments

Notes: ____________________

Total Cost: __________

BREWING

Step 1: Mash

❑ Single-Infusion ❑ Step-Infusion ❑ Decoction

Strike Water Amount: __________ Strike Water Temp: __________°

Starting Mash Temp: __________° Final Mash Temp: __________°

Sparge Water Amount: __________ Sparge Water Temp: __________°

Sparge Temp: __________°

Pre-boil Gravity: __________

Notes: ____

____

For Extract Batches

Water Volume: __________

Grains Steeped for: __________ minutes at __________°

Extract(s) Added: ❑ Start of Boil ❑ __________ Minutes into Boil

Step 2: Boil

Hops & Other Ingredients Schedule

	Time
1. ______________________________	________
2. ______________________________	________
3. ______________________________	________
4. ______________________________	________
5. ______________________________	________
6. ______________________________	________

Step 3: Chilling and Pitching

Chill Method: ❑ Ice Bath ❑ Immersion Coil ❑ __________

Chill Start Time: __________

Chill Finish Time: __________

Original Gravity: __________

Wort Temp at Pitching: __________°

Wort Volume: __________

Aeration Method: ❑ Agitation ❑ Forced

Notes: ______________________________

FERMENTATION

Primary Start Date/Time: ______

❑ Glass Carboy ❑ Plastic Bucket ❑ ______

❑ Airlock ❑ Blow-off Tube ❑ ______

Date/Time: ______ Temp: ______°

Date/Time: ______ Temp: ______°

Date/Time: ______ Temp: ______°

Date/Time: ______ Temp: ______°

Date/Time: ______ Temp: ______°

Date/Time: ______ Temp: ______°

Date/Time: ______ Temp: ______°

Date/Time: ______ Temp: ______°

Additions to Primary or Secondary: ______

Secondary Start Date/Time: ______

Date/Time: ______ Temp: ______°

Date/Time: ______ Temp: ______°

Date/Time: ______ Temp: ______°

Date/Time: ______ Temp: ______°

Date/Time: ______ Temp: ______°

Date/Time: ______ Temp: ______°

Date/Time: ______ Temp: ______°

Date/Time: ______ Temp: ______°

Notes: ______

PACKAGING

Date/Time: ______

Final Gravity: ______

(______ OG – ______ FG) × 131 = ______% ABV

❑ Bottle ❑ Keg

Priming Agent: ______

Amount: ______

-or-

CO_2 Setting: ______ psi for ______ days

Sanitizing Agent/Method: ______

STORAGE/AGING

Date/Time: ______ Temp: ______°

Date/Time: ______ Temp: ______°

Date/Time: ______ Temp: ______°

Date/Time: ______ Temp: ______°

Date/Time: ______ Temp: ______°

Date/Time: ______ Temp: ______°

Notes: ______

FIRST TASTING

Date/Time: ______

Tasters: ______

Glassware: ______

Serving Temp: ______°

Appearance: ______

Aroma: ______

Flavor: ______

Finish: ______

FINAL THOUGHTS

BEER INFO

Beer Name: ______________________

____

Style: ______________________

Brewer(s): ______________________

____

❑ Partial Mash/Extract ❑ All-Grain

Preliminary Notes and Expectations

Gallons: ______________________

OG/FG: ______________________

ABV: ______________________

IBU: ______________________

SRM: ______________________

BREWING DAY

Date: ______________________

Start Time: ______________________

Beer(s) Imbibed: ______________________

____

____

____

____

____

Soundtrack: ______________________

____

____

____

____

____

INGREDIENTS

Grain Bill & Fermentables

	Amount	Cost
1.		
2.		
3.		
4.		
5.		
6.		
7.		
8.		

Hop Bill

	Amount	AA%	Cost
1.			
2.			
3.			
4.			
5.			
6.			

Other Ingredients

	Amount	Cost
1.		
2.		
3.		

Yeast

Variety: ______________________ Cost: __________

Water Adjustments

Notes: ______________________

Total Cost: __________

BREWING

Step 1: Mash

❑ Single-Infusion ❑ Step-Infusion ❑ Decoction

Strike Water Amount: ________ Strike Water Temp: ________°

Starting Mash Temp: ________° Final Mash Temp: ________°

Sparge Water Amount: ________ Sparge Water Temp: ________°

Sparge Temp: ________°

Pre-boil Gravity: ________

Notes: ____

____

For Extract Batches

Water Volume: ________

Grains Steeped for: ________ minutes at ________°

Extract(s) Added: ❑ Start of Boil ❑ ________ Minutes into Boil

Step 2: Boil

Hops & Other Ingredients Schedule

	Time
1. ________________________	________
2. ________________________	________
3. ________________________	________
4. ________________________	________
5. ________________________	________
6. ________________________	________

Step 3: Chilling and Pitching

Chill Method: ❑ Ice Bath ❑ Immersion Coil ❑ ________

Chill Start Time: ________

Chill Finish Time: ________

Original Gravity: ________

Wort Temp at Pitching: ________°

Wort Volume: ________

Aeration Method: ❑ Agitation ❑ Forced

Notes: ____

FERMENTATION

Primary Start Date/Time: ____________________

❑ Glass Carboy ❑ Plastic Bucket ❑ ____________

❑ Airlock ❑ Blow-off Tube ❑ ____________

Date/Time: ____________________ Temp: ________°

Date/Time: ____________________ Temp: ________°

Date/Time: ____________________ Temp: ________°

Date/Time: ____________________ Temp: ________°

Date/Time: ____________________ Temp: ________°

Date/Time: ____________________ Temp: ________°

Date/Time: ____________________ Temp: ________°

Date/Time: ____________________ Temp: ________°

Additions to Primary or Secondary: ____________________

Secondary Start Date/Time: ____________________

Date/Time: ____________________ Temp: ________°

Date/Time: ____________________ Temp: ________°

Date/Time: ____________________ Temp: ________°

Date/Time: ____________________ Temp: ________°

Date/Time: ____________________ Temp: ________°

Date/Time: ____________________ Temp: ________°

Date/Time: ____________________ Temp: ________°

Date/Time: ____________________ Temp: ________°

Notes: ____________________

PACKAGING

Date/Time: ____________________

Final Gravity: ____________________

(_____ OG – _____ FG) × 131 = _____% ABV

❑ Bottle ❑ Keg

Priming Agent: ____________________

Amount: ____________________

-or-

CO_2 Setting: ________ psi for _____ days

Sanitizing Agent/Method: ____________________

STORAGE/AGING

Date/Time: ________ Temp: ________°

Date/Time: ________ Temp: ________°

Date/Time: ________ Temp: ________°

Date/Time: ________ Temp: ________°

Date/Time: ________ Temp: ________°

Date/Time: ________ Temp: ________°

Notes: ____________________

FIRST TASTING

Date/Time:

Tasters:

Glassware:

Serving Temp: °

Appearance:

Aroma:

Flavor:

Finish:

FINAL THOUGHTS

BEER INFO

Beer Name: ______________________

____

Style: ______________________

Brewer(s): ______________________

____

❑ Partial Mash/Extract ❑ All-Grain

Preliminary Notes and Expectations

Gallons: ______________________

OG/FG: ______________________

ABV: ______________________

IBU: ______________________

SRM: ______________________

BREWING DAY

Date: ______________________

Start Time: ______________________

Beer(s) Imbibed: ______________________

____

____

____

____

____

Soundtrack: ______________________

____

____

____

____

____

INGREDIENTS

Grain Bill & Fermentables

	Amount	Cost
1.		
2.		
3.		
4.		
5.		
6.		
7.		
8.		

Hop Bill

	Amount	AA%	Cost
1.			
2.			
3.			
4.			
5.			
6.			

Other Ingredients

	Amount	Cost
1.		
2.		
3.		

Yeast

Variety: ______________________ Cost: __________

Water Adjustments

Notes: ______________________

Total Cost: __________

BREWING

Step 1: Mash

❑ Single-Infusion ❑ Step-Infusion ❑ Decoction

Strike Water Amount: ________ Strike Water Temp: ________°

Starting Mash Temp: ________° Final Mash Temp: ________°

Sparge Water Amount: ________ Sparge Water Temp: ________°

Sparge Temp: ________°

Pre-boil Gravity: ________

Notes: ____

____

For Extract Batches

Water Volume: ________

Grains Steeped for: ________ minutes at ________°

Extract(s) Added: ❑ Start of Boil ❑ ________ Minutes into Boil

Step 2: Boil

Hops & Other Ingredients Schedule

		Time
1.	________________________	________
2.	________________________	________
3.	________________________	________
4.	________________________	________
5.	________________________	________
6.	________________________	________

Step 3: Chilling and Pitching

Chill Method: ❑ Ice Bath ❑ Immersion Coil ❑ ________

Chill Start Time: ________

Chill Finish Time: ________

Original Gravity: ________

Wort Temp at Pitching: ________°

Wort Volume: ________

Aeration Method: ❑ Agitation ❑ Forced

Notes: ____

FERMENTATION

Primary Start Date/Time: ______

❑ Glass Carboy ❑ Plastic Bucket ❑ ______

❑ Airlock ❑ Blow-off Tube ❑ ______

Date/Time: ______ Temp: ______°

Date/Time: ______ Temp: ______°

Date/Time: ______ Temp: ______°

Date/Time: ______ Temp: ______°

Date/Time: ______ Temp: ______°

Date/Time: ______ Temp: ______°

Date/Time: ______ Temp: ______°

Date/Time: ______ Temp: ______°

Additions to Primary or Secondary: ______

Secondary Start Date/Time: ______

Date/Time: ______ Temp: ______°

Date/Time: ______ Temp: ______°

Date/Time: ______ Temp: ______°

Date/Time: ______ Temp: ______°

Date/Time: ______ Temp: ______°

Date/Time: ______ Temp: ______°

Date/Time: ______ Temp: ______°

Date/Time: ______ Temp: ______°

Notes: ______

PACKAGING

Date/Time: ______

Final Gravity: ______

(____ OG – ____ FG) × 131 = ____% ABV

❑ Bottle ❑ Keg

Priming Agent: ______

Amount: ______

-or-

CO_2 Setting: ______ psi for ____ days

Sanitizing Agent/Method: ______

STORAGE/AGING

Date/Time: ______ Temp: ______°

Date/Time: ______ Temp: ______°

Date/Time: ______ Temp: ______°

Date/Time: ______ Temp: ______°

Date/Time: ______ Temp: ______°

Date/Time: ______ Temp: ______°

Notes: ______

FIRST TASTING

Date/Time: ______

Tasters: ______

Glassware: ______

Serving Temp: ______°

Appearance: ______

Aroma: ______

Flavor: ______

Finish: ______

FINAL THOUGHTS

BEER INFO

Beer Name: ______________________

____

Style: ______________________

Brewer(s): ______________________

____

❑ Partial Mash/Extract ❑ All-Grain

Preliminary Notes and Expectations

Gallons: ______________________

OG/FG: ______________________

ABV: ______________________

IBU: ______________________

SRM: ______________________

BREWING DAY

Date: ______________________

Start Time: ______________________

Beer(s) Imbibed: ______________________

____

____

____

____

____

Soundtrack: ______________________

____

____

____

____

____

INGREDIENTS

Grain Bill & Fermentables

	Amount	Cost
1.		
2.		
3.		
4.		
5.		
6.		
7.		
8.		

Hop Bill

	Amount	AA%	Cost
1.			
2.			
3.			
4.			
5.			
6.			

Other Ingredients

	Amount	Cost
1.		
2.		
3.		

Yeast

Variety: ______________________ Cost: __________

Water Adjustments

Notes: ______________________

Total Cost: __________

BREWING

Step 1: Mash

❑ Single-Infusion ❑ Step-Infusion ❑ Decoction

Strike Water Amount: ________ Strike Water Temp: ________°

Starting Mash Temp: ________° Final Mash Temp: ________°

Sparge Water Amount: ________ Sparge Water Temp: ________°

Sparge Temp: ________°

Pre-boil Gravity: ________

Notes: ____

____

For Extract Batches

Water Volume: ________

Grains Steeped for: ________ minutes at ________°

Extract(s) Added: ❑ Start of Boil ❑ ________ Minutes into Boil

Step 2: Boil

Hops & Other Ingredients Schedule

	Time
1. ________________	________
2. ________________	________
3. ________________	________
4. ________________	________
5. ________________	________
6. ________________	________

Step 3: Chilling and Pitching

Chill Method: ❑ Ice Bath ❑ Immersion Coil ❑ ________

Chill Start Time: ________

Chill Finish Time: ________

Original Gravity: ________

Wort Temp at Pitching: ________°

Wort Volume: ________

Aeration Method: ❑ Agitation ❑ Forced

Notes: ____

FERMENTATION

Primary Start Date/Time: ____________

❑ Glass Carboy ❑ Plastic Bucket ❑ ____________

❑ Airlock ❑ Blow-off Tube ❑ ____________

Date/Time: ____________ Temp: ______°

Date/Time: ____________ Temp: ______°

Date/Time: ____________ Temp: ______°

Date/Time: ____________ Temp: ______°

Date/Time: ____________ Temp: ______°

Date/Time: ____________ Temp: ______°

Date/Time: ____________ Temp: ______°

Date/Time: ____________ Temp: ______°

Additions to Primary or Secondary: ____________

Secondary Start Date/Time: ____________

Date/Time: ____________ Temp: ______°

Date/Time: ____________ Temp: ______°

Date/Time: ____________ Temp: ______°

Date/Time: ____________ Temp: ______°

Date/Time: ____________ Temp: ______°

Date/Time: ____________ Temp: ______°

Date/Time: ____________ Temp: ______°

Date/Time: ____________ Temp: ______°

Notes: ____________

PACKAGING

Date/Time: ____________

Final Gravity: ____________

(____ OG – ____ FG) × 131 = ____% ABV

❑ Bottle ❑ Keg

Priming Agent: ____________

Amount: ____________

-or-

CO_2 Setting: ________ psi for ____ days

Sanitizing Agent/Method: ____________

STORAGE/AGING

Date/Time: ________ Temp: ______°

Date/Time: ________ Temp: ______°

Date/Time: ________ Temp: ______°

Date/Time: ________ Temp: ______°

Date/Time: ________ Temp: ______°

Date/Time: ________ Temp: ______°

Notes: ____________

FIRST TASTING

Date/Time: ________________________________

Tasters: ________________________________

Glassware: ________________________________

Serving Temp: ________°

Appearance: ________________________________

Aroma: ________________________________

Flavor: ________________________________

Finish: ________________________________

FINAL THOUGHTS

BEER INFO

Beer Name: ____________________

____

Style: ____________________

Brewer(s): ____________________

____

❑ Partial Mash/Extract ❑ All-Grain

Preliminary Notes and Expectations

Gallons: ____________________

OG/FG: ____________________

ABV: ____________________

IBU: ____________________

SRM: ____________________

BREWING DAY

Date: ____________________

Start Time: ____________________

Beer(s) Imbibed: ____________________

____

____

____

____

____

Soundtrack: ____________________

____

____

____

____

____

INGREDIENTS

Grain Bill & Fermentables

	Amount	Cost
1.		
2.		
3.		
4.		
5.		
6.		
7.		
8.		

Hop Bill

	Amount	AA%	Cost
1.			
2.			
3.			
4.			
5.			
6.			

Other Ingredients

	Amount	Cost
1.		
2.		
3.		

Yeast

Variety: ____________________ Cost: __________

Water Adjustments

Notes: ____________________

Total Cost: __________

BREWING

STEP 1: Mash

❑ Single-Infusion ❑ Step-Infusion ❑ Decoction

Strike Water Amount: __________ Strike Water Temp: __________°

Starting Mash Temp: __________° Final Mash Temp: __________°

Sparge Water Amount: __________ Sparge Water Temp: __________°

Sparge Temp: __________°

Pre-boil Gravity: __________

Notes: ____

____

For Extract Batches

Water Volume: __________

Grains Steeped for: __________ minutes at __________°

Extract(s) Added: ❑ Start of Boil ❑ __________ Minutes into Boil

STEP 2: Boil

Hops & Other Ingredients Schedule

		Time
1.	______________________________	__________
2.	______________________________	__________
3.	______________________________	__________
4.	______________________________	__________
5.	______________________________	__________
6.	______________________________	__________

STEP 3: Chilling and Pitching

Chill Method: ❑ Ice Bath ❑ Immersion Coil ❑ __________

Chill Start Time: __________

Chill Finish Time: __________

Original Gravity: __________

Wort Temp at Pitching: __________°

Wort Volume: __________

Aeration Method: ❑ Agitation ❑ Forced

Notes: ______________________________

FERMENTATION

Primary Start Date/Time: ______

❑ Glass Carboy ❑ Plastic Bucket ❑ ______

❑ Airlock ❑ Blow-off Tube ❑ ______

Date/Time: ______ Temp: ______°

Date/Time: ______ Temp: ______°

Date/Time: ______ Temp: ______°

Date/Time: ______ Temp: ______°

Date/Time: ______ Temp: ______°

Date/Time: ______ Temp: ______°

Date/Time: ______ Temp: ______°

Date/Time: ______ Temp: ______°

Additions to Primary or Secondary: ______

Secondary Start Date/Time: ______

Date/Time: ______ Temp: ______°

Date/Time: ______ Temp: ______°

Date/Time: ______ Temp: ______°

Date/Time: ______ Temp: ______°

Date/Time: ______ Temp: ______°

Date/Time: ______ Temp: ______°

Date/Time: ______ Temp: ______°

Date/Time: ______ Temp: ______°

Notes: ______

PACKAGING

Date/Time: ______

Final Gravity: ______

(____ OG – ____ FG) × 131 = ____% ABV

❑ Bottle ❑ Keg

Priming Agent: ______

Amount: ______

-or-

CO_2 Setting: ______ psi for ____ days

Sanitizing Agent/Method: ______

STORAGE/AGING

Date/Time: ______ Temp: ______°

Date/Time: ______ Temp: ______°

Date/Time: ______ Temp: ______°

Date/Time: ______ Temp: ______°

Date/Time: ______ Temp: ______°

Date/Time: ______ Temp: ______°

Notes: ______

FIRST TASTING

Date/Time: ____

Tasters: ____

Glassware: ____

Serving Temp: __________°

Appearance: ____

Aroma: ____

Flavor: ____

Finish: ____

FINAL THOUGHTS

BEER INFO

Beer Name: ________________________

____

Style: ________________________

Brewer(s): ________________________

____

❑ Partial Mash/Extract ❑ All-Grain

Preliminary Notes and Expectations

Gallons: ________________________

OG/FG: ________________________

ABV: ________________________

IBU: ________________________

SRM: ________________________

BREWING DAY

Date: ________________________

Start Time: ________________________

Beer(s) Imbibed: ________________________

____

____

____

____

____

Soundtrack: ________________________

____

____

____

____

____

INGREDIENTS

Grain Bill & Fermentables

	Amount	Cost
1.		
2.		
3.		
4.		
5.		
6.		
7.		
8.		

Hop Bill

	Amount	AA%	Cost
1.			
2.			
3.			
4.			
5.			
6.			

Other Ingredients

	Amount	Cost
1.		
2.		
3.		

Yeast

Variety: ________________________ Cost: ________

Water Adjustments

Notes: ________________________

Total Cost: ________

BREWING

Step 1: Mash

❑ Single-Infusion ❑ Step-Infusion ❑ Decoction

Strike Water Amount: ________ Strike Water Temp: ________°

Starting Mash Temp: ________° Final Mash Temp: ________°

Sparge Water Amount: ________ Sparge Water Temp: ________°

Sparge Temp: ________°

Pre-boil Gravity: ________

Notes: ____

____

For Extract Batches

Water Volume: ________

Grains Steeped for: ________ minutes at ________°

Extract(s) Added: ❑ Start of Boil ❑ ________ Minutes into Boil

Step 2: Boil

Hops & Other Ingredients Schedule

	Time
1. ________________________	________
2. ________________________	________
3. ________________________	________
4. ________________________	________
5. ________________________	________
6. ________________________	________

Step 3: Chilling and Pitching

Chill Method: ❑ Ice Bath ❑ Immersion Coil ❑ ________

Chill Start Time: ________

Chill Finish Time: ________

Original Gravity: ________

Wort Temp at Pitching: ________°

Wort Volume: ________

Aeration Method: ❑ Agitation ❑ Forced

Notes: ____

FERMENTATION

Primary Start Date/Time: ____

❑ Glass Carboy ❑ Plastic Bucket ❑ ____

❑ Airlock ❑ Blow-off Tube ❑ ____

Date/Time: ____ Temp: ____°

Date/Time: ____ Temp: ____°

Date/Time: ____ Temp: ____°

Date/Time: ____ Temp: ____°

Date/Time: ____ Temp: ____°

Date/Time: ____ Temp: ____°

Date/Time: ____ Temp: ____°

Date/Time: ____ Temp: ____°

Additions to Primary or Secondary: ____

Secondary Start Date/Time: ____

Date/Time: ____ Temp: ____°

Date/Time: ____ Temp: ____°

Date/Time: ____ Temp: ____°

Date/Time: ____ Temp: ____°

Date/Time: ____ Temp: ____°

Date/Time: ____ Temp: ____°

Date/Time: ____ Temp: ____°

Date/Time: ____ Temp: ____°

Notes: ____

PACKAGING

Date/Time: ____

Final Gravity: ____

(____ OG – ____ FG) × 131 = ____% ABV

❑ Bottle ❑ Keg

Priming Agent: ____

Amount: ____

-or-

CO_2 Setting: ____ psi for ____ days

Sanitizing Agent/Method: ____

STORAGE/AGING

Date/Time: ____ Temp: ____°

Date/Time: ____ Temp: ____°

Date/Time: ____ Temp: ____°

Date/Time: ____ Temp: ____°

Date/Time: ____ Temp: ____°

Date/Time: ____ Temp: ____°

Notes: ____

FIRST TASTING

Date/Time: ______

Tasters: ______

Glassware: ______

Serving Temp: ______°

Appearance: ______

Aroma: ______

Flavor: ______

Finish: ______

FINAL THOUGHTS

BEER INFO

Beer Name: ______________________

____

Style: ______________________

Brewer(s): ______________________

____

❑ Partial Mash/Extract ❑ All-Grain

Preliminary Notes and Expectations

Gallons: ______________________

OG/FG: ______________________

ABV: ______________________

IBU: ______________________

SRM: ______________________

BREWING DAY

Date: ______________________

Start Time: ______________________

Beer(s) Imbibed: ______________________

____

____

____

____

____

Soundtrack: ______________________

____

____

____

____

____

INGREDIENTS

Grain Bill & Fermentables

	Amount	Cost
1.		
2.		
3.		
4.		
5.		
6.		
7.		
8.		

Hop Bill

	Amount	AA%	Cost
1.			
2.			
3.			
4.			
5.			
6.			

Other Ingredients

	Amount	Cost
1.		
2.		
3.		

Yeast

Variety: ______________________ Cost: __________

Water Adjustments

Notes: ______________________

Total Cost: __________

BREWING

Step 1: Mash

❑ Single-Infusion ❑ Step-Infusion ❑ Decoction

Strike Water Amount: __________ Strike Water Temp: __________°

Starting Mash Temp: __________° Final Mash Temp: __________°

Sparge Water Amount: __________ Sparge Water Temp: __________°

Sparge Temp: __________°

Pre-boil Gravity: __________

Notes: ____

____

For Extract Batches

Water Volume: __________

Grains Steeped for: __________ minutes at __________°

Extract(s) Added: ❑ Start of Boil ❑ __________ Minutes into Boil

Step 2: Boil

Hops & Other Ingredients Schedule

		Time
1.	____________________	______
2.	____________________	______
3.	____________________	______
4.	____________________	______
5.	____________________	______
6.	____________________	______

Step 3: Chilling and Pitching

Chill Method: ❑ Ice Bath ❑ Immersion Coil ❑ __________

Chill Start Time: __________

Chill Finish Time: __________

Original Gravity: __________

Wort Temp at Pitching: __________°

Wort Volume: __________

Aeration Method: ❑ Agitation ❑ Forced

Notes: ____

FERMENTATION

Primary Start Date/Time: ____________________

❑ Glass Carboy ❑ Plastic Bucket ❑ ____________

❑ Airlock ❑ Blow-off Tube ❑ ____________

Date/Time: ____________ Temp: ______°

Date/Time: ____________ Temp: ______°

Date/Time: ____________ Temp: ______°

Date/Time: ____________ Temp: ______°

Date/Time: ____________ Temp: ______°

Date/Time: ____________ Temp: ______°

Date/Time: ____________ Temp: ______°

Date/Time: ____________ Temp: ______°

Additions to Primary or Secondary: ____________________

Secondary Start Date/Time: ____________________

Date/Time: ____________ Temp: ______°

Date/Time: ____________ Temp: ______°

Date/Time: ____________ Temp: ______°

Date/Time: ____________ Temp: ______°

Date/Time: ____________ Temp: ______°

Date/Time: ____________ Temp: ______°

Date/Time: ____________ Temp: ______°

Date/Time: ____________ Temp: ______°

Notes: ____________________

PACKAGING

Date/Time: ____________________

Final Gravity: ____________________

(_____ OG – _____ FG) × 131 = _____% ABV

❑ Bottle ❑ Keg

Priming Agent: ____________________

Amount: ____________________

-or-

CO_2 Setting: ________ psi for _____ days

Sanitizing Agent/Method: ____________________

STORAGE/AGING

Date/Time: ________ Temp: ______°

Date/Time: ________ Temp: ______°

Date/Time: ________ Temp: ______°

Date/Time: ________ Temp: ______°

Date/Time: ________ Temp: ______°

Date/Time: ________ Temp: ______°

Notes: ____________________

FIRST TASTING

Date/Time: ______

Tasters: ______

Glassware: ______

Serving Temp: ______°

Appearance: ______

Aroma: ______

Flavor: ______

Finish: ______

FINAL THOUGHTS

BEER INFO

Beer Name: ____________________

____

Style: ____________________

Brewer(s): ____________________

____

❑ Partial Mash/Extract ❑ All-Grain

Preliminary Notes and Expectations

Gallons: ____________________

OG/FG: ____________________

ABV: ____________________

IBU: ____________________

SRM: ____________________

BREWING DAY

Date: ____________________

Start Time: ____________________

Beer(s) Imbibed: ____________________

____

____

____

____

____

Soundtrack: ____________________

____

____

____

____

____

INGREDIENTS

Grain Bill & Fermentables

	Amount	Cost
1.		
2.		
3.		
4.		
5.		
6.		
7.		
8.		

Hop Bill

	Amount	AA%	Cost
1.			
2.			
3.			
4.			
5.			
6.			

Other Ingredients

	Amount	Cost
1.		
2.		
3.		

Yeast

Variety: ____________________ Cost: ________

Water Adjustments

Notes: ____________________

Total Cost: ________

BREWING

Step 1: Mash

❑ Single-Infusion ❑ Step-Infusion ❑ Decoction

Strike Water Amount: ________ Strike Water Temp: ________°

Starting Mash Temp: ________° Final Mash Temp: ________°

Sparge Water Amount: ________ Sparge Water Temp: ________°

Sparge Temp: ________°

Pre-boil Gravity: ________

Notes: ____

____

For Extract Batches

Water Volume: ________

Grains Steeped for: ________ minutes at ________°

Extract(s) Added: ❑ Start of Boil ❑ ________ Minutes into Boil

Step 2: Boil

Hops & Other Ingredients Schedule

	Time
1. ________________________________	________
2. ________________________________	________
3. ________________________________	________
4. ________________________________	________
5. ________________________________	________
6. ________________________________	________

Step 3: Chilling and Pitching

Chill Method: ❑ Ice Bath ❑ Immersion Coil ❑ ________

Chill Start Time: ________

Chill Finish Time: ________

Original Gravity: ________

Wort Temp at Pitching: ________°

Wort Volume: ________

Aeration Method: ❑ Agitation ❑ Forced

Notes: ____

FERMENTATION

Primary Start Date/Time: ______________________

❑ Glass Carboy ❑ Plastic Bucket ❑ ____________

❑ Airlock ❑ Blow-off Tube ❑ ____________

Date/Time: ______________________ Temp: ______°

Date/Time: ______________________ Temp: ______°

Date/Time: ______________________ Temp: ______°

Date/Time: ______________________ Temp: ______°

Date/Time: ______________________ Temp: ______°

Date/Time: ______________________ Temp: ______°

Date/Time: ______________________ Temp: ______°

Date/Time: ______________________ Temp: ______°

Additions to Primary or Secondary: ______________________

Secondary Start Date/Time: ______________________

Date/Time: ______________________ Temp: ______°

Date/Time: ______________________ Temp: ______°

Date/Time: ______________________ Temp: ______°

Date/Time: ______________________ Temp: ______°

Date/Time: ______________________ Temp: ______°

Date/Time: ______________________ Temp: ______°

Date/Time: ______________________ Temp: ______°

Date/Time: ______________________ Temp: ______°

Notes: ______________________

PACKAGING

Date/Time: ______________________

Final Gravity: ______________________

(_____ OG – _____ FG) × 131 = _____% ABV

❑ Bottle ❑ Keg

Priming Agent: ______________________

Amount: ______________________

-or-

CO_2 Setting: __________ psi for _____ days

Sanitizing Agent/Method: ______________________

STORAGE/AGING

Date/Time: __________ Temp: ______°

Date/Time: __________ Temp: ______°

Date/Time: __________ Temp: ______°

Date/Time: __________ Temp: ______°

Date/Time: __________ Temp: ______°

Date/Time: __________ Temp: ______°

Notes: ______________________

FIRST TASTING

Date/Time: ____________________

Tasters: ____________________

Glassware: ____________________

Serving Temp: ________°

Appearance: ____________________

Aroma: ____________________

Flavor: ____________________

Finish: ____________________

FINAL THOUGHTS

BEER INFO

Beer Name: ______

Style: ______

Brewer(s): ______

❑ Partial Mash/Extract ❑ All-Grain

Preliminary Notes and Expectations

Gallons: ______

OG/FG: ______

ABV: ______

IBU: ______

SRM: ______

BREWING DAY

Date: ______

Start Time: ______

Beer(s) Imbibed: ______

Soundtrack: ______

INGREDIENTS

Grain Bill & Fermentables

	Amount	Cost
1.		
2.		
3.		
4.		
5.		
6.		
7.		
8.		

Hop Bill

	Amount	AA%	Cost
1.			
2.			
3.			
4.			
5.			
6.			

Other Ingredients

	Amount	Cost
1.		
2.		
3.		

Yeast

Variety: ______ Cost: ______

Water Adjustments

Notes: ______

Total Cost: ______

BREWING

Step 1: Mash

❑ Single-Infusion ❑ Step-Infusion ❑ Decoction

Strike Water Amount: __________ Strike Water Temp: __________°

Starting Mash Temp: __________° Final Mash Temp: __________°

Sparge Water Amount: __________ Sparge Water Temp: __________°

Sparge Temp: __________°

Pre-boil Gravity: __________

Notes: ____

____

For Extract Batches

Water Volume: __________

Grains Steeped for: __________ minutes at __________°

Extract(s) Added: ❑ Start of Boil ❑ __________ Minutes into Boil

Step 2: Boil

Hops & Other Ingredients Schedule

	Time
1. ______________________________	________
2. ______________________________	________
3. ______________________________	________
4. ______________________________	________
5. ______________________________	________
6. ______________________________	________

Step 3: Chilling and Pitching

Chill Method: ❑ Ice Bath ❑ Immersion Coil ❑ __________

Chill Start Time: __________

Chill Finish Time: __________

Original Gravity: __________

Wort Temp at Pitching: __________°

Wort Volume: __________

Aeration Method: ❑ Agitation ❑ Forced

Notes: ______________________________

FERMENTATION

Primary Start Date/Time: ______

❑ Glass Carboy ❑ Plastic Bucket ❑ ______

❑ Airlock ❑ Blow-off Tube ❑ ______

Date/Time: ______ Temp: ______°

Date/Time: ______ Temp: ______°

Date/Time: ______ Temp: ______°

Date/Time: ______ Temp: ______°

Date/Time: ______ Temp: ______°

Date/Time: ______ Temp: ______°

Date/Time: ______ Temp: ______°

Date/Time: ______ Temp: ______°

Additions to Primary or Secondary: ______

Secondary Start Date/Time: ______

Date/Time: ______ Temp: ______°

Date/Time: ______ Temp: ______°

Date/Time: ______ Temp: ______°

Date/Time: ______ Temp: ______°

Date/Time: ______ Temp: ______°

Date/Time: ______ Temp: ______°

Date/Time: ______ Temp: ______°

Date/Time: ______ Temp: ______°

Notes: ______

PACKAGING

Date/Time: ______

Final Gravity: ______

(______ OG – ______ FG) × 131 = ______% ABV

❑ Bottle ❑ Keg

Priming Agent: ______

Amount: ______

-or-

CO_2 Setting: ______ psi for ______ days

Sanitizing Agent/Method: ______

STORAGE/AGING

Date/Time: ______ Temp: ______°

Date/Time: ______ Temp: ______°

Date/Time: ______ Temp: ______°

Date/Time: ______ Temp: ______°

Date/Time: ______ Temp: ______°

Date/Time: ______ Temp: ______°

Notes: ______

FIRST TASTING

Date/Time: ______________________________

Tasters: ______________________________

Glassware: ______________________________

Serving Temp: __________°

Appearance: ______________________________

Aroma: ______________________________

Flavor: ______________________________

Finish: ______________________________

FINAL THOUGHTS

BEER INFO

Beer Name: ______________________

____

Style: ______________________

Brewer(s): ______________________

____

❑ Partial Mash/Extract ❑ All-Grain

Preliminary Notes and Expectations

Gallons: ______________________

OG/FG: ______________________

ABV: ______________________

IBU: ______________________

SRM: ______________________

BREWING DAY

Date: ______________________

Start Time: ______________________

Beer(s) Imbibed: ______________________

____

____

____

____

____

Soundtrack: ______________________

____

____

____

____

____

INGREDIENTS

Grain Bill & Fermentables

	Amount	Cost
1.		
2.		
3.		
4.		
5.		
6.		
7.		
8.		

Hop Bill

	Amount	AA%	Cost
1.			
2.			
3.			
4.			
5.			
6.			

Other Ingredients

	Amount	Cost
1.		
2.		
3.		

Yeast

Variety: ______________________ Cost: __________

Water Adjustments

Notes: ______________________

Total Cost: __________

BREWING

Step 1: Mash

☐ Single-Infusion ☐ Step-Infusion ☐ Decoction

Strike Water Amount: ________ Strike Water Temp: ________°

Starting Mash Temp: ________° Final Mash Temp: ________°

Sparge Water Amount: ________ Sparge Water Temp: ________°

Sparge Temp: ________°

Pre-boil Gravity: ________

Notes: ____

____

For Extract Batches

Water Volume: ________

Grains Steeped for: ________ minutes at ________°

Extract(s) Added: ☐ Start of Boil ☐ ________ Minutes into Boil

Step 2: Boil

Hops & Other Ingredients Schedule

	Time
1. ________________________________	________
2. ________________________________	________
3. ________________________________	________
4. ________________________________	________
5. ________________________________	________
6. ________________________________	________

Step 3: Chilling and Pitching

Chill Method: ☐ Ice Bath ☐ Immersion Coil ☐ ________

Chill Start Time: ________

Chill Finish Time: ________

Original Gravity: ________

Wort Temp at Pitching: ________°

Wort Volume: ________

Aeration Method: ☐ Agitation ☐ Forced

Notes: ____

FERMENTATION

Primary Start Date/Time: ____________________

❑ Glass Carboy ❑ Plastic Bucket ❑ ____________

❑ Airlock ❑ Blow-off Tube ❑ ____________

Date/Time: ____________________ Temp: ________°

Date/Time: ____________________ Temp: ________°

Date/Time: ____________________ Temp: ________°

Date/Time: ____________________ Temp: ________°

Date/Time: ____________________ Temp: ________°

Date/Time: ____________________ Temp: ________°

Date/Time: ____________________ Temp: ________°

Date/Time: ____________________ Temp: ________°

Additions to Primary or Secondary: ____________________

Secondary Start Date/Time: ____________________

Date/Time: ____________________ Temp: ________°

Date/Time: ____________________ Temp: ________°

Date/Time: ____________________ Temp: ________°

Date/Time: ____________________ Temp: ________°

Date/Time: ____________________ Temp: ________°

Date/Time: ____________________ Temp: ________°

Date/Time: ____________________ Temp: ________°

Date/Time: ____________________ Temp: ________°

Notes: ____________________

PACKAGING

Date/Time: ____________________

Final Gravity: ____________________

(_____ OG – _____ FG) × 131 = _____% ABV

❑ Bottle ❑ Keg

Priming Agent: ____________________

Amount: ____________________

-or-

CO_2 Setting: __________ psi for _____ days

Sanitizing Agent/Method: ____________________

STORAGE/AGING

Date/Time: __________ Temp: ________°

Date/Time: __________ Temp: ________°

Date/Time: __________ Temp: ________°

Date/Time: __________ Temp: ________°

Date/Time: __________ Temp: ________°

Date/Time: __________ Temp: ________°

Notes: ____________________

FIRST TASTING

Date/Time: ______________________

Tasters: ______________________

Glassware: ______________________

Serving Temp: __________°

Appearance: ______________________

Aroma: ______________________

Flavor: ______________________

Finish: ______________________

FINAL THOUGHTS

BEER INFO

Beer Name: ____________________

____

Style: ____________________

Brewer(s): ____________________

____

❑ Partial Mash/Extract ❑ All-Grain

Preliminary Notes and Expectations

Gallons: ____________________

OG/FG: ____________________

ABV: ____________________

IBU: ____________________

SRM: ____________________

BREWING DAY

Date: ____________________

Start Time: ____________________

Beer(s) Imbibed: ____________________

____

____

____

____

____

Soundtrack: ____________________

____

____

____

____

____

INGREDIENTS

Grain Bill & Fermentables

	Amount	Cost
1.		
2.		
3.		
4.		
5.		
6.		
7.		
8.		

Hop Bill

	Amount	AA%	Cost
1.			
2.			
3.			
4.			
5.			
6.			

Other Ingredients

	Amount	Cost
1.		
2.		
3.		

Yeast

Variety: ____________________ Cost: __________

Water Adjustments

Notes: ____________________

Total Cost: __________

BREWING

Step 1: Mash

❑ Single-Infusion ❑ Step-Infusion ❑ Decoction

Strike Water Amount: ________ Strike Water Temp: ________°

Starting Mash Temp: ________° Final Mash Temp: ________°

Sparge Water Amount: ________ Sparge Water Temp: ________°

Sparge Temp: ________°

Pre-boil Gravity: ________

Notes: ____

____

For Extract Batches

Water Volume: ________

Grains Steeped for: ________ minutes at ________°

Extract(s) Added: ❑ Start of Boil ❑ ________ Minutes into Boil

Step 2: Boil

Hops & Other Ingredients Schedule

	Time
1. ________________________________	________
2. ________________________________	________
3. ________________________________	________
4. ________________________________	________
5. ________________________________	________
6. ________________________________	________

Step 3: Chilling and Pitching

Chill Method: ❑ Ice Bath ❑ Immersion Coil ❑ ________

Chill Start Time: ________

Chill Finish Time: ________

Original Gravity: ________

Wort Temp at Pitching: ________°

Wort Volume: ________

Aeration Method: ❑ Agitation ❑ Forced

Notes: ________________________________

FERMENTATION

Primary Start Date/Time: ____________________

❑ Glass Carboy ❑ Plastic Bucket ❑ ____________

❑ Airlock ❑ Blow-off Tube ❑ ____________

Date/Time: ____________ Temp: ______°

Date/Time: ____________ Temp: ______°

Date/Time: ____________ Temp: ______°

Date/Time: ____________ Temp: ______°

Date/Time: ____________ Temp: ______°

Date/Time: ____________ Temp: ______°

Date/Time: ____________ Temp: ______°

Date/Time: ____________ Temp: ______°

Additions to Primary or Secondary: ____________________

Secondary Start Date/Time: ____________________

Date/Time: ____________ Temp: ______°

Date/Time: ____________ Temp: ______°

Date/Time: ____________ Temp: ______°

Date/Time: ____________ Temp: ______°

Date/Time: ____________ Temp: ______°

Date/Time: ____________ Temp: ______°

Date/Time: ____________ Temp: ______°

Date/Time: ____________ Temp: ______°

Notes: ____________________

PACKAGING

Date/Time: ____________________

Final Gravity: ____________________

(____ OG – ____ FG) × 131 = ____% ABV

❑ Bottle ❑ Keg

Priming Agent: ____________________

Amount: ____________________

-or-

CO_2 Setting: ________ psi for ____ days

Sanitizing Agent/Method: ____________________

STORAGE/AGING

Date/Time: ________ Temp: ______°

Date/Time: ________ Temp: ______°

Date/Time: ________ Temp: ______°

Date/Time: ________ Temp: ______°

Date/Time: ________ Temp: ______°

Date/Time: ________ Temp: ______°

Notes: ____________________

FIRST TASTING

Date/Time: ____________________

Tasters: ____________________

Glassware: ____________________

Serving Temp: __________°

Appearance: ____________________

Aroma: ____________________

Flavor: ____________________

Finish: ____________________

FINAL THOUGHTS

BEER INFO

Beer Name: ____________________

____

Style: ____________________

Brewer(s): ____________________

____

❑ Partial Mash/Extract ❑ All-Grain

Preliminary Notes and Expectations

Gallons: ____________________

OG/FG: ____________________

ABV: ____________________

IBU: ____________________

SRM: ____________________

BREWING DAY

Date: ____________________

Start Time: ____________________

Beer(s) Imbibed: ____________________

____

____

____

____

____

Soundtrack: ____________________

____

____

____

____

____

INGREDIENTS

Grain Bill & Fermentables

	Amount	Cost
1.		
2.		
3.		
4.		
5.		
6.		
7.		
8.		

Hop Bill

	Amount	AA%	Cost
1.			
2.			
3.			
4.			
5.			
6.			

Other Ingredients

	Amount	Cost
1.		
2.		
3.		

Yeast

Variety: ____________________ Cost: ________

Water Adjustments

Notes: ____________________

Total Cost: ________

BREWING

Step 1: Mash

❑ Single-Infusion ❑ Step-Infusion ❑ Decoction

Strike Water Amount: __________ Strike Water Temp: __________°

Starting Mash Temp: __________° Final Mash Temp: __________°

Sparge Water Amount: __________ Sparge Water Temp: __________°

Sparge Temp: __________°

Pre-boil Gravity: __________

Notes: ____

____

For Extract Batches

Water Volume: __________

Grains Steeped for: __________ minutes at __________°

Extract(s) Added: ❑ Start of Boil ❑ __________ Minutes into Boil

Step 2: Boil

Hops & Other Ingredients Schedule

	Time
1. ____________________	______
2. ____________________	______
3. ____________________	______
4. ____________________	______
5. ____________________	______
6. ____________________	______

Step 3: Chilling and Pitching

Chill Method: ❑ Ice Bath ❑ Immersion Coil ❑ __________

Chill Start Time: __________

Chill Finish Time: __________

Original Gravity: __________

Wort Temp at Pitching: __________°

Wort Volume: __________

Aeration Method: ❑ Agitation ❑ Forced

Notes: ____________________

FERMENTATION

Primary Start Date/Time: ______

❑ Glass Carboy ❑ Plastic Bucket ❑ ______

❑ Airlock ❑ Blow-off Tube ❑ ______

Date/Time: ______ Temp: ______°

Date/Time: ______ Temp: ______°

Date/Time: ______ Temp: ______°

Date/Time: ______ Temp: ______°

Date/Time: ______ Temp: ______°

Date/Time: ______ Temp: ______°

Date/Time: ______ Temp: ______°

Date/Time: ______ Temp: ______°

Additions to Primary or Secondary: ______

______

______

______

______

Secondary Start Date/Time: ______

Date/Time: ______ Temp: ______°

Date/Time: ______ Temp: ______°

Date/Time: ______ Temp: ______°

Date/Time: ______ Temp: ______°

Date/Time: ______ Temp: ______°

Date/Time: ______ Temp: ______°

Date/Time: ______ Temp: ______°

Date/Time: ______ Temp: ______°

Notes: ______

______

______

______

______

PACKAGING

Date/Time: ______

Final Gravity: ______

(____ OG – ____ FG) × 131 = ____% ABV

❑ Bottle ❑ Keg

Priming Agent: ______

Amount: ______

-or-

CO_2 Setting: ______ psi for ____ days

Sanitizing Agent/Method: ______

______

______

STORAGE/AGING

Date/Time: ______ Temp: ______°

Date/Time: ______ Temp: ______°

Date/Time: ______ Temp: ______°

Date/Time: ______ Temp: ______°

Date/Time: ______ Temp: ______°

Date/Time: ______ Temp: ______°

Notes: ______

______

______

______

______

______

______

______

______

______

FIRST TASTING

Date/Time: ______

Tasters: ______

Glassware: ______

Serving Temp: ______°

Appearance: ______

Aroma: ______

Flavor: ______

Finish: ______

FINAL THOUGHTS

BEER INFO

Beer Name: ____________________

____

Style: ____________________

Brewer(s): ____________________

____

❑ Partial Mash/Extract ❑ All-Grain

Preliminary Notes and Expectations

Gallons: ____________________

OG/FG: ____________________

ABV: ____________________

IBU: ____________________

SRM: ____________________

BREWING DAY

Date: ____________________

Start Time: ____________________

Beer(s) Imbibed: ____________________

____

____

____

____

____

Soundtrack: ____________________

____

____

____

____

____

INGREDIENTS

Grain Bill & Fermentables

	Amount	Cost
1.		
2.		
3.		
4.		
5.		
6.		
7.		
8.		

Hop Bill

	Amount	AA%	Cost
1.			
2.			
3.			
4.			
5.			
6.			

Other Ingredients

	Amount	Cost
1.		
2.		
3.		

Yeast

Variety: ____________________ Cost: ________

Water Adjustments

Notes: ____________________

Total Cost: ________

BREWING

Step 1: Mash

❑ Single-Infusion ❑ Step-Infusion ❑ Decoction

Strike Water Amount: ________ Strike Water Temp: ________°

Starting Mash Temp: ________° Final Mash Temp: ________°

Sparge Water Amount: ________ Sparge Water Temp: ________°

Sparge Temp: ________°

Pre-boil Gravity: ________

Notes: ____

____

For Extract Batches

Water Volume: ________

Grains Steeped for: ________ minutes at ________°

Extract(s) Added: ❑ Start of Boil ❑ ________ Minutes into Boil

Step 2: Boil

Hops & Other Ingredients Schedule

	Time
1. ________________________________	________
2. ________________________________	________
3. ________________________________	________
4. ________________________________	________
5. ________________________________	________
6. ________________________________	________

Step 3: Chilling and Pitching

Chill Method: ❑ Ice Bath ❑ Immersion Coil ❑ ________

Chill Start Time: ________

Chill Finish Time: ________

Original Gravity: ________

Wort Temp at Pitching: ________°

Wort Volume: ________

Aeration Method: ❑ Agitation ❑ Forced

Notes: ____

FERMENTATION

Primary Start Date/Time: ______

❑ Glass Carboy ❑ Plastic Bucket ❑ ______

❑ Airlock ❑ Blow-off Tube ❑ ______

Date/Time: ______ Temp: ______°

Date/Time: ______ Temp: ______°

Date/Time: ______ Temp: ______°

Date/Time: ______ Temp: ______°

Date/Time: ______ Temp: ______°

Date/Time: ______ Temp: ______°

Date/Time: ______ Temp: ______°

Date/Time: ______ Temp: ______°

Additions to Primary or Secondary: ______

______

______

______

______

Secondary Start Date/Time: ______

Date/Time: ______ Temp: ______°

Date/Time: ______ Temp: ______°

Date/Time: ______ Temp: ______°

Date/Time: ______ Temp: ______°

Date/Time: ______ Temp: ______°

Date/Time: ______ Temp: ______°

Date/Time: ______ Temp: ______°

Date/Time: ______ Temp: ______°

Notes: ______

______

______

______

______

PACKAGING

Date/Time: ______

Final Gravity: ______

(______ OG – ______ FG) × 131 = ______% ABV

❑ Bottle ❑ Keg

Priming Agent: ______

Amount: ______

-or-

CO_2 Setting: ______ psi for ______ days

Sanitizing Agent/Method: ______

______

______

STORAGE/AGING

Date/Time: ______ Temp: ______°

Date/Time: ______ Temp: ______°

Date/Time: ______ Temp: ______°

Date/Time: ______ Temp: ______°

Date/Time: ______ Temp: ______°

Date/Time: ______ Temp: ______°

Notes: ______

______

______

______

______

______

______

______

______

______

FIRST TASTING

Date/Time: __________

Tasters: __________

Glassware: __________

Serving Temp: ______°

Appearance: __________

Aroma: __________

Flavor: __________

Finish: __________

FINAL THOUGHTS

BEER INFO

Beer Name: ______________________

____

Style: ______________________

Brewer(s): ______________________

____

❑ Partial Mash/Extract ❑ All-Grain

Preliminary Notes and Expectations

Gallons: ______________________

OG/FG: ______________________

ABV: ______________________

IBU: ______________________

SRM: ______________________

BREWING DAY

Date: ______________________

Start Time: ______________________

Beer(s) Imbibed: ______________________

____

____

____

____

____

Soundtrack: ______________________

____

____

____

____

____

INGREDIENTS

Grain Bill & Fermentables

	Amount	Cost
1.		
2.		
3.		
4.		
5.		
6.		
7.		
8.		

Hop Bill

	Amount	AA%	Cost
1.			
2.			
3.			
4.			
5.			
6.			

Other Ingredients

	Amount	Cost
1.		
2.		
3.		

Yeast

Variety: ______________________ Cost: ________

Water Adjustments

Notes: ______________________

Total Cost: ________

BREWING

STEP 1: Mash

❑ Single-Infusion ❑ Step-Infusion ❑ Decoction

Strike Water Amount: ________ Strike Water Temp: ________°

Starting Mash Temp: ________° Final Mash Temp: ________°

Sparge Water Amount: ________ Sparge Water Temp: ________°

Sparge Temp: ________°

Pre-boil Gravity: ________

Notes: ____

____

For Extract Batches

Water Volume: ________

Grains Steeped for: ________ minutes at ________°

Extract(s) Added: ❑ Start of Boil ❑ ________ Minutes into Boil

STEP 2: Boil

Hops & Other Ingredients Schedule

	Time
1. ________________________________	________
2. ________________________________	________
3. ________________________________	________
4. ________________________________	________
5. ________________________________	________
6. ________________________________	________

STEP 3: Chilling and Pitching

Chill Method: ❑ Ice Bath ❑ Immersion Coil ❑ ________

Chill Start Time: ________

Chill Finish Time: ________

Original Gravity: ________

Wort Temp at Pitching: ________°

Wort Volume: ________

Aeration Method: ❑ Agitation ❑ Forced

Notes: ____

FERMENTATION

Primary Start Date/Time: ______

❑ Glass Carboy ❑ Plastic Bucket ❑ ______

❑ Airlock ❑ Blow-off Tube ❑ ______

Date/Time: ______ Temp: ______°

Date/Time: ______ Temp: ______°

Date/Time: ______ Temp: ______°

Date/Time: ______ Temp: ______°

Date/Time: ______ Temp: ______°

Date/Time: ______ Temp: ______°

Date/Time: ______ Temp: ______°

Date/Time: ______ Temp: ______°

Additions to Primary or Secondary: ______

Secondary Start Date/Time: ______

Date/Time: ______ Temp: ______°

Date/Time: ______ Temp: ______°

Date/Time: ______ Temp: ______°

Date/Time: ______ Temp: ______°

Date/Time: ______ Temp: ______°

Date/Time: ______ Temp: ______°

Date/Time: ______ Temp: ______°

Date/Time: ______ Temp: ______°

Notes: ______

PACKAGING

Date/Time: ______

Final Gravity: ______

(______ OG – ______ FG) × 131 = ______% ABV

❑ Bottle ❑ Keg

Priming Agent: ______

Amount: ______

-or-

CO_2 Setting: ______ psi for ______ days

Sanitizing Agent/Method: ______

STORAGE/AGING

Date/Time: ______ Temp: ______°

Date/Time: ______ Temp: ______°

Date/Time: ______ Temp: ______°

Date/Time: ______ Temp: ______°

Date/Time: ______ Temp: ______°

Date/Time: ______ Temp: ______°

Notes: ______

FIRST TASTING

Date/Time: ____________________

Tasters: ____________________

Glassware: ____________________

Serving Temp: __________°

Appearance: ____________________

Aroma: ____________________

Flavor: ____________________

Finish: ____________________

FINAL THOUGHTS

BEER INFO

Beer Name: ______________________

____

Style: ______________________

Brewer(s): ______________________

____

❑ Partial Mash/Extract ❑ All-Grain

Preliminary Notes and Expectations

Gallons: ______________________

OG/FG: ______________________

ABV: ______________________

IBU: ______________________

SRM: ______________________

BREWING DAY

Date: ______________________

Start Time: ______________________

Beer(s) Imbibed: ______________________

____

____

____

____

____

Soundtrack: ______________________

____

____

____

____

____

INGREDIENTS

Grain Bill & Fermentables

	Amount	Cost
1.		
2.		
3.		
4.		
5.		
6.		
7.		
8.		

Hop Bill

	Amount	AA%	Cost
1.			
2.			
3.			
4.			
5.			
6.			

Other Ingredients

	Amount	Cost
1.		
2.		
3.		

Yeast

Variety: ______________________ Cost: ________

Water Adjustments

Notes: ______________________

Total Cost: ________

BREWING

Step 1: Mash

❑ Single-Infusion ❑ Step-Infusion ❑ Decoction

Strike Water Amount: ________ Strike Water Temp: ________°

Starting Mash Temp: ________° Final Mash Temp: ________°

Sparge Water Amount: ________ Sparge Water Temp: ________°

Sparge Temp: ________°

Pre-boil Gravity: ________

Notes: ____

____

For Extract Batches

Water Volume: ________

Grains Steeped for: ________ minutes at ________°

Extract(s) Added: ❑ Start of Boil ❑ ________ Minutes into Boil

Step 2: Boil

Hops & Other Ingredients Schedule

	Time
1. ________________________	________
2. ________________________	________
3. ________________________	________
4. ________________________	________
5. ________________________	________
6. ________________________	________

Step 3: Chilling and Pitching

Chill Method: ❑ Ice Bath ❑ Immersion Coil ❑ ________

Chill Start Time: ________

Chill Finish Time: ________

Original Gravity: ________

Wort Temp at Pitching: ________°

Wort Volume: ________

Aeration Method: ❑ Agitation ❑ Forced

Notes: ________________________

FERMENTATION

Primary Start Date/Time: ______________________

❑ Glass Carboy ❑ Plastic Bucket ❑ ______________

❑ Airlock ❑ Blow-off Tube ❑ ______________

Date/Time: ______________ Temp: ______°

Date/Time: ______________ Temp: ______°

Date/Time: ______________ Temp: ______°

Date/Time: ______________ Temp: ______°

Date/Time: ______________ Temp: ______°

Date/Time: ______________ Temp: ______°

Date/Time: ______________ Temp: ______°

Date/Time: ______________ Temp: ______°

Additions to Primary or Secondary: ______________

Secondary Start Date/Time: ______________________

Date/Time: ______________ Temp: ______°

Date/Time: ______________ Temp: ______°

Date/Time: ______________ Temp: ______°

Date/Time: ______________ Temp: ______°

Date/Time: ______________ Temp: ______°

Date/Time: ______________ Temp: ______°

Date/Time: ______________ Temp: ______°

Date/Time: ______________ Temp: ______°

Notes: ______________

PACKAGING

Date/Time: ______________

Final Gravity: ______________

(_____ OG – _____ FG) × 131 = _____% ABV

❑ Bottle ❑ Keg

Priming Agent: ______________

Amount: ______________

-or-

CO_2 Setting: ________ psi for _____ days

Sanitizing Agent/Method: ______________

STORAGE/AGING

Date/Time: ________ Temp: ______°

Date/Time: ________ Temp: ______°

Date/Time: ________ Temp: ______°

Date/Time: ________ Temp: ______°

Date/Time: ________ Temp: ______°

Date/Time: ________ Temp: ______°

Notes: ______________

FIRST TASTING

Date/Time: ____________________

Tasters: ____________________

Glassware: ____________________

Serving Temp: __________°

Appearance: ____________________

Aroma: ____________________

Flavor: ____________________

Finish: ____________________

FINAL THOUGHTS

BEER INFO

Beer Name: ____________________

____

Style: ____________________

Brewer(s): ____________________

____

❑ Partial Mash/Extract ❑ All-Grain

Preliminary Notes and Expectations

Gallons: ____________________

OG/FG: ____________________

ABV: ____________________

IBU: ____________________

SRM: ____________________

BREWING DAY

Date: ____________________

Start Time: ____________________

Beer(s) Imbibed: ____________________

____

____

____

____

____

Soundtrack: ____________________

____

____

____

____

____

INGREDIENTS

Grain Bill & Fermentables

	Amount	Cost
1.		
2.		
3.		
4.		
5.		
6.		
7.		
8.		

Hop Bill

	Amount	AA%	Cost
1.			
2.			
3.			
4.			
5.			
6.			

Other Ingredients

	Amount	Cost
1.		
2.		
3.		

Yeast

Variety: ____________________ Cost: __________

Water Adjustments

Notes: ____________________

Total Cost: __________

BREWING

Step 1: Mash

☐ Single-Infusion ☐ Step-Infusion ☐ Decoction

Strike Water Amount: ________ Strike Water Temp: ________°

Starting Mash Temp: ________° Final Mash Temp: ________°

Sparge Water Amount: ________ Sparge Water Temp: ________°

Sparge Temp: ________°

Pre-boil Gravity: ________

Notes: ____

____

For Extract Batches

Water Volume: ________

Grains Steeped for: ________ minutes at ________°

Extract(s) Added: ☐ Start of Boil ☐ ________ Minutes into Boil

Step 2: Boil

Hops & Other Ingredients Schedule

	Time
1. ________________	________
2. ________________	________
3. ________________	________
4. ________________	________
5. ________________	________
6. ________________	________

Step 3: Chilling and Pitching

Chill Method: ☐ Ice Bath ☐ Immersion Coil ☐ ________

Chill Start Time: ________

Chill Finish Time: ________

Original Gravity: ________

Wort Temp at Pitching: ________°

Wort Volume: ________

Aeration Method: ☐ Agitation ☐ Forced

Notes: ____

FERMENTATION

Primary Start Date/Time: ____________________

❑ Glass Carboy ❑ Plastic Bucket ❑ ____________

❑ Airlock ❑ Blow-off Tube ❑ ____________

Date/Time: ____________________ Temp: ________°

Date/Time: ____________________ Temp: ________°

Date/Time: ____________________ Temp: ________°

Date/Time: ____________________ Temp: ________°

Date/Time: ____________________ Temp: ________°

Date/Time: ____________________ Temp: ________°

Date/Time: ____________________ Temp: ________°

Date/Time: ____________________ Temp: ________°

Additions to Primary or Secondary: ____________________

Secondary Start Date/Time: ____________________

Date/Time: ____________________ Temp: ________°

Date/Time: ____________________ Temp: ________°

Date/Time: ____________________ Temp: ________°

Date/Time: ____________________ Temp: ________°

Date/Time: ____________________ Temp: ________°

Date/Time: ____________________ Temp: ________°

Date/Time: ____________________ Temp: ________°

Date/Time: ____________________ Temp: ________°

Notes: ____________________

PACKAGING

Date/Time: ____________________

Final Gravity: ____________________

(_____ OG – _____ FG) × 131 = _____% ABV

❑ Bottle ❑ Keg

Priming Agent: ____________________

Amount: ____________________

-or-

CO_2 Setting: __________ psi for _____ days

Sanitizing Agent/Method: ____________________

STORAGE/AGING

Date/Time: __________ Temp: ________°

Date/Time: __________ Temp: ________°

Date/Time: __________ Temp: ________°

Date/Time: __________ Temp: ________°

Date/Time: __________ Temp: ________°

Date/Time: __________ Temp: ________°

Notes: ____________________

FIRST TASTING

Date/Time: ___

Tasters: ___

Glassware: ___

Serving Temp: ___°

Appearance: ___

Aroma: ___

Flavor: ___

Finish: ___

FINAL THOUGHTS

BEER INFO

Beer Name: ______________________

____

Style: ______________________

Brewer(s): ______________________

____

❑ Partial Mash/Extract ❑ All-Grain

Preliminary Notes and Expectations

Gallons: ______________________

OG/FG: ______________________

ABV: ______________________

IBU: ______________________

SRM: ______________________

BREWING DAY

Date: ______________________

Start Time: ______________________

Beer(s) Imbibed: ______________________

____

____

____

____

____

Soundtrack: ______________________

____

____

____

____

____

INGREDIENTS

Grain Bill & Fermentables

	Amount	Cost
1.		
2.		
3.		
4.		
5.		
6.		
7.		
8.		

Hop Bill

	Amount	AA%	Cost
1.			
2.			
3.			
4.			
5.			
6.			

Other Ingredients

	Amount	Cost
1.		
2.		
3.		

Yeast

Variety: ______________________ Cost: __________

Water Adjustments

Notes: ______________________

Total Cost: __________

BREWING

Step 1: Mash

❑ Single-Infusion ❑ Step-Infusion ❑ Decoction

Strike Water Amount: ________ Strike Water Temp: ________°

Starting Mash Temp: ________° Final Mash Temp: ________°

Sparge Water Amount: ________ Sparge Water Temp: ________°

Sparge Temp: ________°

Pre-boil Gravity: ________

Notes: ____

____

For Extract Batches

Water Volume: ________

Grains Steeped for: ________ minutes at ________°

Extract(s) Added: ❑ Start of Boil ❑ ________ Minutes into Boil

Step 2: Boil

Hops & Other Ingredients Schedule

	Time
1. ________________________________	________
2. ________________________________	________
3. ________________________________	________
4. ________________________________	________
5. ________________________________	________
6. ________________________________	________

Step 3: Chilling and Pitching

Chill Method: ❑ Ice Bath ❑ Immersion Coil ❑ ________

Chill Start Time: ________

Chill Finish Time: ________

Original Gravity: ________

Wort Temp at Pitching: ________°

Wort Volume: ________

Aeration Method: ❑ Agitation ❑ Forced

Notes: ____

FERMENTATION

Primary Start Date/Time: ______

❑ Glass Carboy ❑ Plastic Bucket ❑ ______

❑ Airlock ❑ Blow-off Tube ❑ ______

Date/Time: ______ Temp: ______°

Date/Time: ______ Temp: ______°

Date/Time: ______ Temp: ______°

Date/Time: ______ Temp: ______°

Date/Time: ______ Temp: ______°

Date/Time: ______ Temp: ______°

Date/Time: ______ Temp: ______°

Date/Time: ______ Temp: ______°

Additions to Primary or Secondary: ______

______

______

______

______

Secondary Start Date/Time: ______

Date/Time: ______ Temp: ______°

Date/Time: ______ Temp: ______°

Date/Time: ______ Temp: ______°

Date/Time: ______ Temp: ______°

Date/Time: ______ Temp: ______°

Date/Time: ______ Temp: ______°

Date/Time: ______ Temp: ______°

Date/Time: ______ Temp: ______°

Notes: ______

______

______

______

______

PACKAGING

Date/Time: ______

Final Gravity: ______

(______ OG – ______ FG) × 131 = ______% ABV

❑ Bottle ❑ Keg

Priming Agent: ______

Amount: ______

-or-

CO_2 Setting: ______ psi for ______ days

Sanitizing Agent/Method: ______

______

______

STORAGE/AGING

Date/Time: ______ Temp: ______°

Date/Time: ______ Temp: ______°

Date/Time: ______ Temp: ______°

Date/Time: ______ Temp: ______°

Date/Time: ______ Temp: ______°

Date/Time: ______ Temp: ______°

Notes: ______

______

______

______

______

______

______

______

______

______

FIRST TASTING

Date/Time: ____________________

Tasters: ____________________

Glassware: ____________________

Serving Temp: __________°

Appearance: ____________________

Aroma: ____________________

Flavor: ____________________

Finish: ____________________

FINAL THOUGHTS

BEER INFO

Beer Name: ______________________

____

Style: ______________________

Brewer(s): ______________________

____

❑ Partial Mash/Extract ❑ All-Grain

Preliminary Notes and Expectations

Gallons: ______________________

OG/FG: ______________________

ABV: ______________________

IBU: ______________________

SRM: ______________________

BREWING DAY

Date: ______________________

Start Time: ______________________

Beer(s) Imbibed: ______________________

____

____

____

____

____

Soundtrack: ______________________

____

____

____

____

____

INGREDIENTS

Grain Bill & Fermentables

		Amount	Cost
1.			
2.			
3.			
4.			
5.			
6.			
7.			
8.			

Hop Bill

		Amount	AA%	Cost
1.				
2.				
3.				
4.				
5.				
6.				

Other Ingredients

		Amount	Cost
1.			
2.			
3.			

Yeast

Variety: ______________________ Cost: __________

Water Adjustments

Notes: ______________________

Total Cost: __________

BREWING

Step 1: Mash

❏ Single-Infusion ❏ Step-Infusion ❏ Decoction

Strike Water Amount: ________ Strike Water Temp: ________°

Starting Mash Temp: ________° Final Mash Temp: ________°

Sparge Water Amount: ________ Sparge Water Temp: ________°

Sparge Temp: ________°

Pre-boil Gravity: ________

Notes: ________

____

For Extract Batches

Water Volume: ________

Grains Steeped for: ________ minutes at ________°

Extract(s) Added: ❏ Start of Boil ❏ ________ Minutes into Boil

Step 2: Boil

Hops & Other Ingredients Schedule

	Time
1. ________	________
2. ________	________
3. ________	________
4. ________	________
5. ________	________
6. ________	________

Step 3: Chilling and Pitching

Chill Method: ❏ Ice Bath ❏ Immersion Coil ❏ ________

Chill Start Time: ________

Chill Finish Time: ________

Original Gravity: ________

Wort Temp at Pitching: ________°

Wort Volume: ________

Aeration Method: ❏ Agitation ❏ Forced

Notes: ________

FERMENTATION

Primary Start Date/Time: ____________________

❑ Glass Carboy ❑ Plastic Bucket ❑ __________

❑ Airlock ❑ Blow-off Tube ❑ __________

Date/Time: ____________________ Temp: ________°

Date/Time: ____________________ Temp: ________°

Date/Time: ____________________ Temp: ________°

Date/Time: ____________________ Temp: ________°

Date/Time: ____________________ Temp: ________°

Date/Time: ____________________ Temp: ________°

Date/Time: ____________________ Temp: ________°

Date/Time: ____________________ Temp: ________°

Additions to Primary or Secondary: ____________________

Secondary Start Date/Time: ____________________

Date/Time: ____________________ Temp: ________°

Date/Time: ____________________ Temp: ________°

Date/Time: ____________________ Temp: ________°

Date/Time: ____________________ Temp: ________°

Date/Time: ____________________ Temp: ________°

Date/Time: ____________________ Temp: ________°

Date/Time: ____________________ Temp: ________°

Date/Time: ____________________ Temp: ________°

Notes: ____________________

PACKAGING

Date/Time: ____________________

Final Gravity: ____________________

(_____ OG – _____ FG) × 131 = _____% ABV

❑ Bottle ❑ Keg

Priming Agent: ____________________

Amount: ____________________

-or-

CO_2 Setting: __________ psi for _____ days

Sanitizing Agent/Method: ____________________

STORAGE/AGING

Date/Time: __________ Temp: ________°

Date/Time: __________ Temp: ________°

Date/Time: __________ Temp: ________°

Date/Time: __________ Temp: ________°

Date/Time: __________ Temp: ________°

Date/Time: __________ Temp: ________°

Notes: ____________________

FIRST TASTING

Date/Time: ______

Tasters: ______

Glassware: ______

Serving Temp: ______°

Appearance: ______

Aroma: ______

Flavor: ______

Finish: ______

FINAL THOUGHTS

BEER INFO

Beer Name: ______________________

____

Style: ______________________

Brewer(s): ______________________

____

❑ Partial Mash/Extract ❑ All-Grain

Preliminary Notes and Expectations

Gallons: ______________________

OG/FG: ______________________

ABV: ______________________

IBU: ______________________

SRM: ______________________

BREWING DAY

Date: ______________________

Start Time: ______________________

Beer(s) Imbibed: ______________________

____

____

____

____

____

Soundtrack: ______________________

____

____

____

____

____

INGREDIENTS

Grain Bill & Fermentables

	Amount	Cost
1.		
2.		
3.		
4.		
5.		
6.		
7.		
8.		

Hop Bill

	Amount	AA%	Cost
1.			
2.			
3.			
4.			
5.			
6.			

Other Ingredients

	Amount	Cost
1.		
2.		
3.		

Yeast

Variety: ______________________ Cost: __________

Water Adjustments

Notes: ______________________

Total Cost: __________

BREWING

Step 1: Mash

❑ Single-Infusion ❑ Step-Infusion ❑ Decoction

Strike Water Amount: __________ Strike Water Temp: __________°

Starting Mash Temp: __________° Final Mash Temp: __________°

Sparge Water Amount: __________ Sparge Water Temp: __________°

Sparge Temp: __________°

Pre-boil Gravity: __________

Notes: ____

____

For Extract Batches

Water Volume: __________

Grains Steeped for: __________ minutes at __________°

Extract(s) Added: ❑ Start of Boil ❑ __________ Minutes into Boil

Step 2: Boil

Hops & Other Ingredients Schedule

		Time
1.	____________________	______
2.	____________________	______
3.	____________________	______
4.	____________________	______
5.	____________________	______
6.	____________________	______

Step 3: Chilling and Pitching

Chill Method: ❑ Ice Bath ❑ Immersion Coil ❑ __________

Chill Start Time: __________

Chill Finish Time: __________

Original Gravity: __________

Wort Temp at Pitching: __________°

Wort Volume: __________

Aeration Method: ❑ Agitation ❑ Forced

Notes: ____

FERMENTATION

Primary Start Date/Time: ______

❑ Glass Carboy ❑ Plastic Bucket ❑ ______

❑ Airlock ❑ Blow-off Tube ❑ ______

Date/Time: ______ Temp: ______°

Date/Time: ______ Temp: ______°

Date/Time: ______ Temp: ______°

Date/Time: ______ Temp: ______°

Date/Time: ______ Temp: ______°

Date/Time: ______ Temp: ______°

Date/Time: ______ Temp: ______°

Date/Time: ______ Temp: ______°

Additions to Primary or Secondary: ______

______

______

______

______

Secondary Start Date/Time: ______

Date/Time: ______ Temp: ______°

Date/Time: ______ Temp: ______°

Date/Time: ______ Temp: ______°

Date/Time: ______ Temp: ______°

Date/Time: ______ Temp: ______°

Date/Time: ______ Temp: ______°

Date/Time: ______ Temp: ______°

Date/Time: ______ Temp: ______°

Notes: ______

______

______

______

______

PACKAGING

Date/Time: ______

Final Gravity: ______

(____ OG – ____ FG) × 131 = ____% ABV

❑ Bottle ❑ Keg

Priming Agent: ______

Amount: ______

-or-

CO_2 Setting: ______ psi for ____ days

Sanitizing Agent/Method: ______

______

______

STORAGE/AGING

Date/Time: ______ Temp: ______°

Date/Time: ______ Temp: ______°

Date/Time: ______ Temp: ______°

Date/Time: ______ Temp: ______°

Date/Time: ______ Temp: ______°

Date/Time: ______ Temp: ______°

Notes: ______

______

______

______

______

______

______

______

______

______

FIRST TASTING

Date/Time: ______________________

Tasters: ______________________

Glassware: ______________________

Serving Temp: __________°

Appearance: ______________________

Aroma: ______________________

Flavor: ______________________

Finish: ______________________

FINAL THOUGHTS

BEER INFO

Beer Name: ______________________

____

Style: ______________________

Brewer(s): ______________________

____

❑ Partial Mash/Extract ❑ All-Grain

Preliminary Notes and Expectations

Gallons: ______________________

OG/FG: ______________________

ABV: ______________________

IBU: ______________________

SRM: ______________________

BREWING DAY

Date: ______________________

Start Time: ______________________

Beer(s) Imbibed: ______________________

____

____

____

____

____

Soundtrack: ______________________

____

____

____

____

____

INGREDIENTS

Grain Bill & Fermentables

	Amount	Cost
1.		
2.		
3.		
4.		
5.		
6.		
7.		
8.		

Hop Bill

	Amount	AA%	Cost
1.			
2.			
3.			
4.			
5.			
6.			

Other Ingredients

	Amount	Cost
1.		
2.		
3.		

Yeast

Variety: ______________________ Cost: __________

Water Adjustments

Notes: ______________________

Total Cost: __________

STEP 1: Mash

❑ Single-Infusion ❑ Step-Infusion ❑ Decoction

Strike Water Amount: ________ Strike Water Temp: ________°

Starting Mash Temp: ________° Final Mash Temp: ________°

Sparge Water Amount: ________ Sparge Water Temp: ________°

Sparge Temp: ________°

Pre-boil Gravity: ________

Notes: ____

____

For Extract Batches

Water Volume: ________

Grains Steeped for: ________ minutes at ________°

Extract(s) Added: ❑ Start of Boil ❑ ________ Minutes into Boil

STEP 2: Boil

Hops & Other Ingredients Schedule

		Time
1.	________________________________	________
2.	________________________________	________
3.	________________________________	________
4.	________________________________	________
5.	________________________________	________
6.	________________________________	________

STEP 3: Chilling and Pitching

Chill Method: ❑ Ice Bath ❑ Immersion Coil ❑ ________

Chill Start Time: ________

Chill Finish Time: ________

Original Gravity: ________

Wort Temp at Pitching: ________°

Wort Volume: ________

Aeration Method: ❑ Agitation ❑ Forced

Notes: ____

FERMENTATION

Primary Start Date/Time: ______

❑ Glass Carboy ❑ Plastic Bucket ❑ ______

❑ Airlock ❑ Blow-off Tube ❑ ______

Date/Time: ______ Temp: ______°

Date/Time: ______ Temp: ______°

Date/Time: ______ Temp: ______°

Date/Time: ______ Temp: ______°

Date/Time: ______ Temp: ______°

Date/Time: ______ Temp: ______°

Date/Time: ______ Temp: ______°

Date/Time: ______ Temp: ______°

Additions to Primary or Secondary: ______

______

______

______

______

Secondary Start Date/Time: ______

Date/Time: ______ Temp: ______°

Date/Time: ______ Temp: ______°

Date/Time: ______ Temp: ______°

Date/Time: ______ Temp: ______°

Date/Time: ______ Temp: ______°

Date/Time: ______ Temp: ______°

Date/Time: ______ Temp: ______°

Date/Time: ______ Temp: ______°

Notes: ______

______

______

______

______

PACKAGING

Date/Time: ______

Final Gravity: ______

(______ OG – ______ FG) × 131 = ______% ABV

❑ Bottle ❑ Keg

Priming Agent: ______

Amount: ______

-or-

CO_2 Setting: ______ psi for ______ days

Sanitizing Agent/Method: ______

______

______

STORAGE/AGING

Date/Time: ______ Temp: ______°

Date/Time: ______ Temp: ______°

Date/Time: ______ Temp: ______°

Date/Time: ______ Temp: ______°

Date/Time: ______ Temp: ______°

Date/Time: ______ Temp: ______°

Notes: ______

______

______

______

______

______

______

______

______

______

FIRST TASTING

Date/Time: ______

Tasters: ______

Glassware: ______

Serving Temp: ______°

Appearance: ______

Aroma: ______

Flavor: ______

Finish: ______

FINAL THOUGHTS

BEER INFO

Beer Name: ______________________

____

Style: ______________________

Brewer(s): ______________________

____

❑ Partial Mash/Extract ❑ All-Grain

Preliminary Notes and Expectations

Gallons: ______________________

OG/FG: ______________________

ABV: ______________________

IBU: ______________________

SRM: ______________________

BREWING DAY

Date: ______________________

Start Time: ______________________

Beer(s) Imbibed: ______________________

____

____

____

____

____

Soundtrack: ______________________

____

____

____

____

____

INGREDIENTS

Grain Bill & Fermentables

	Amount	Cost
1.		
2.		
3.		
4.		
5.		
6.		
7.		
8.		

Hop Bill

	Amount	AA%	Cost
1.			
2.			
3.			
4.			
5.			
6.			

Other Ingredients

	Amount	Cost
1.		
2.		
3.		

Yeast

Variety: ______________________ Cost: ________

Water Adjustments

Notes: ______________________

Total Cost: ________

BREWING

Step 1: Mash

❑ Single-Infusion ❑ Step-Infusion ❑ Decoction

Strike Water Amount: __________ Strike Water Temp: __________°

Starting Mash Temp: __________° Final Mash Temp: __________°

Sparge Water Amount: __________ Sparge Water Temp: __________°

Sparge Temp: __________°

Pre-boil Gravity: __________

Notes: ____

____

For Extract Batches

Water Volume: __________

Grains Steeped for: __________ minutes at __________°

Extract(s) Added: ❑ Start of Boil ❑ __________ Minutes into Boil

Step 2: Boil

Hops & Other Ingredients Schedule

	Time
1. ______________________________	__________
2. ______________________________	__________
3. ______________________________	__________
4. ______________________________	__________
5. ______________________________	__________
6. ______________________________	__________

Step 3: Chilling and Pitching

Chill Method: ❑ Ice Bath ❑ Immersion Coil ❑ __________

Chill Start Time: __________

Chill Finish Time: __________

Original Gravity: __________

Wort Temp at Pitching: __________°

Wort Volume: __________

Aeration Method: ❑ Agitation ❑ Forced

Notes: ____________________________

FERMENTATION

Primary Start Date/Time: ______________________

❑ Glass Carboy ❑ Plastic Bucket ❑ ______________

❑ Airlock ❑ Blow-off Tube ❑ ______________

Date/Time: ______________ Temp: ______°

Date/Time: ______________ Temp: ______°

Date/Time: ______________ Temp: ______°

Date/Time: ______________ Temp: ______°

Date/Time: ______________ Temp: ______°

Date/Time: ______________ Temp: ______°

Date/Time: ______________ Temp: ______°

Date/Time: ______________ Temp: ______°

Additions to Primary or Secondary: ______________

Secondary Start Date/Time: ______________________

Date/Time: ______________ Temp: ______°

Date/Time: ______________ Temp: ______°

Date/Time: ______________ Temp: ______°

Date/Time: ______________ Temp: ______°

Date/Time: ______________ Temp: ______°

Date/Time: ______________ Temp: ______°

Date/Time: ______________ Temp: ______°

Date/Time: ______________ Temp: ______°

Notes: ______________

PACKAGING

Date/Time: ______________

Final Gravity: ______________

(_____ OG – _____ FG) × 131 = _____% ABV

❑ Bottle ❑ Keg

Priming Agent: ______________

Amount: ______________

-or-

CO_2 Setting: ________ psi for _____ days

Sanitizing Agent/Method: ______________

STORAGE/AGING

Date/Time: ________ Temp: ______°

Date/Time: ________ Temp: ______°

Date/Time: ________ Temp: ______°

Date/Time: ________ Temp: ______°

Date/Time: ________ Temp: ______°

Date/Time: ________ Temp: ______°

Notes: ______________

FIRST TASTING

Date/Time: ________________________

Tasters: ________________________

Glassware: ________________________

Serving Temp: ________ °

Appearance: ________________________

Aroma: ________________________

Flavor: ________________________

Finish: ________________________

FINAL THOUGHTS

BEER INFO

Beer Name: ______________________

____

Style: ______________________

Brewer(s): ______________________

____

❑ Partial Mash/Extract ❑ All-Grain

Preliminary Notes and Expectations

Gallons: ______________________

OG/FG: ______________________

ABV: ______________________

IBU: ______________________

SRM: ______________________

BREWING DAY

Date: ______________________

Start Time: ______________________

Beer(s) Imbibed: ______________________

____

____

____

____

____

Soundtrack: ______________________

____

____

____

____

____

INGREDIENTS

Grain Bill & Fermentables

	Amount	Cost
1.		
2.		
3.		
4.		
5.		
6.		
7.		
8.		

Hop Bill

	Amount	AA%	Cost
1.			
2.			
3.			
4.			
5.			
6.			

Other Ingredients

	Amount	Cost
1.		
2.		
3.		

Yeast

Variety: ______________________ Cost: __________

Water Adjustments

Notes: ______________________

Total Cost: __________

BREWING

Step 1: Mash

❑ Single-Infusion ❑ Step-Infusion ❑ Decoction

Strike Water Amount: ________ Strike Water Temp: ________°

Starting Mash Temp: ________° Final Mash Temp: ________°

Sparge Water Amount: ________ Sparge Water Temp: ________°

Sparge Temp: ________°

Pre-boil Gravity: ________

Notes: ____

____

For Extract Batches

Water Volume: ________

Grains Steeped for: ________ minutes at ________°

Extract(s) Added: ❑ Start of Boil ❑ ________ Minutes into Boil

Step 2: Boil

Hops & Other Ingredients Schedule

	Time
1. ________________________________	________
2. ________________________________	________
3. ________________________________	________
4. ________________________________	________
5. ________________________________	________
6. ________________________________	________

Step 3: Chilling and Pitching

Chill Method: ❑ Ice Bath ❑ Immersion Coil ❑ ________

Chill Start Time: ________

Chill Finish Time: ________

Original Gravity: ________

Wort Temp at Pitching: ________°

Wort Volume: ________

Aeration Method: ❑ Agitation ❑ Forced

Notes: ________________________________

FERMENTATION

Primary Start Date/Time: ______

❑ Glass Carboy ❑ Plastic Bucket ❑ ______

❑ Airlock ❑ Blow-off Tube ❑ ______

Date/Time: ______ Temp: ______°

Date/Time: ______ Temp: ______°

Date/Time: ______ Temp: ______°

Date/Time: ______ Temp: ______°

Date/Time: ______ Temp: ______°

Date/Time: ______ Temp: ______°

Date/Time: ______ Temp: ______°

Date/Time: ______ Temp: ______°

Additions to Primary or Secondary: ______

Secondary Start Date/Time: ______

Date/Time: ______ Temp: ______°

Date/Time: ______ Temp: ______°

Date/Time: ______ Temp: ______°

Date/Time: ______ Temp: ______°

Date/Time: ______ Temp: ______°

Date/Time: ______ Temp: ______°

Date/Time: ______ Temp: ______°

Date/Time: ______ Temp: ______°

Notes: ______

PACKAGING

Date/Time: ______

Final Gravity: ______

(______ OG – ______ FG) × 131 = ______% ABV

❑ Bottle ❑ Keg

Priming Agent: ______

Amount: ______

-or-

CO_2 Setting: ______ psi for ______ days

Sanitizing Agent/Method: ______

STORAGE/AGING

Date/Time: ______ Temp: ______°

Date/Time: ______ Temp: ______°

Date/Time: ______ Temp: ______°

Date/Time: ______ Temp: ______°

Date/Time: ______ Temp: ______°

Date/Time: ______ Temp: ______°

Notes: ______

FIRST TASTING

Date/Time: ______________________

Tasters: ______________________

Glassware: ______________________

Serving Temp: __________°

Appearance: ______________________

Aroma: ______________________

Flavor: ______________________

Finish: ______________________

FINAL THOUGHTS

BEER INFO

Beer Name: ____________________

____

Style: ____________________

Brewer(s): ____________________

____

❏ Partial Mash/Extract ❏ All-Grain

Preliminary Notes and Expectations

Gallons: ____________________

OG/FG: ____________________

ABV: ____________________

IBU: ____________________

SRM: ____________________

BREWING DAY

Date: ____________________

Start Time: ____________________

Beer(s) Imbibed: ____________________

____

____

____

____

____

Soundtrack: ____________________

____

____

____

____

____

INGREDIENTS

Grain Bill & Fermentables

	Amount	Cost
1.		
2.		
3.		
4.		
5.		
6.		
7.		
8.		

Hop Bill

	Amount	AA%	Cost
1.			
2.			
3.			
4.			
5.			
6.			

Other Ingredients

	Amount	Cost
1.		
2.		
3.		

Yeast

Variety: ____________________ Cost: __________

Water Adjustments

Notes: ____________________

Total Cost: __________

BREWING

Step 1: Mash

❑ Single-Infusion ❑ Step-Infusion ❑ Decoction

Strike Water Amount: ________ Strike Water Temp: ________°

Starting Mash Temp: ________° Final Mash Temp: ________°

Sparge Water Amount: ________ Sparge Water Temp: ________°

Sparge Temp: ________°

Pre-boil Gravity: ________

Notes: ____

____

For Extract Batches

Water Volume: ________

Grains Steeped for: ________ minutes at ________°

Extract(s) Added: ❑ Start of Boil ❑ ________ Minutes into Boil

Step 2: Boil

Hops & Other Ingredients Schedule

		Time
1.	________	________
2.	________	________
3.	________	________
4.	________	________
5.	________	________
6.	________	________

Step 3: Chilling and Pitching

Chill Method: ❑ Ice Bath ❑ Immersion Coil ❑ ________

Chill Start Time: ________

Chill Finish Time: ________

Original Gravity: ________

Wort Temp at Pitching: ________°

Wort Volume: ________

Aeration Method: ❑ Agitation ❑ Forced

Notes: ____

FERMENTATION

Primary Start Date/Time: ____________________

❑ Glass Carboy ❑ Plastic Bucket ❑ ____________

❑ Airlock ❑ Blow-off Tube ❑ ____________

Date/Time: ____________ Temp: ______°

Date/Time: ____________ Temp: ______°

Date/Time: ____________ Temp: ______°

Date/Time: ____________ Temp: ______°

Date/Time: ____________ Temp: ______°

Date/Time: ____________ Temp: ______°

Date/Time: ____________ Temp: ______°

Date/Time: ____________ Temp: ______°

Additions to Primary or Secondary: ____________________

Secondary Start Date/Time: ____________________

Date/Time: ____________ Temp: ______°

Date/Time: ____________ Temp: ______°

Date/Time: ____________ Temp: ______°

Date/Time: ____________ Temp: ______°

Date/Time: ____________ Temp: ______°

Date/Time: ____________ Temp: ______°

Date/Time: ____________ Temp: ______°

Date/Time: ____________ Temp: ______°

Notes: ____________________

PACKAGING

Date/Time: ____________________

Final Gravity: ____________________

(_____ OG – _____ FG) × 131 = _____% ABV

❑ Bottle ❑ Keg

Priming Agent: ____________________

Amount: ____________________

-or-

CO_2 Setting: ________ psi for _____ days

Sanitizing Agent/Method: ____________________

STORAGE/AGING

Date/Time: ________ Temp: ______°

Date/Time: ________ Temp: ______°

Date/Time: ________ Temp: ______°

Date/Time: ________ Temp: ______°

Date/Time: ________ Temp: ______°

Date/Time: ________ Temp: ______°

Notes: ____________________

FIRST TASTING

Date/Time: ______________________

Tasters: ______________________

Glassware: ______________________

Serving Temp: ________°

Appearance: ______________________

Aroma: ______________________

Flavor: ______________________

Finish: ______________________

FINAL THOUGHTS

BEER INFO

Beer Name: ______________________

____

Style: ______________________

Brewer(s): ______________________

____

❑ Partial Mash/Extract ❑ All-Grain

Preliminary Notes and Expectations

Gallons: ______________________

OG/FG: ______________________

ABV: ______________________

IBU: ______________________

SRM: ______________________

BREWING DAY

Date: ______________________

Start Time: ______________________

Beer(s) Imbibed: ______________________

____

____

____

____

____

Soundtrack: ______________________

____

____

____

____

____

INGREDIENTS

Grain Bill & Fermentables

	Amount	Cost
1.		
2.		
3.		
4.		
5.		
6.		
7.		
8.		

Hop Bill

	Amount	AA%	Cost
1.			
2.			
3.			
4.			
5.			
6.			

Other Ingredients

	Amount	Cost
1.		
2.		
3.		

Yeast

Variety: ______________________ Cost: ________

Water Adjustments

Notes: ______________________

Total Cost: ________

BREWING

Step 1: Mash

❑ Single-Infusion ❑ Step-Infusion ❑ Decoction

Strike Water Amount: ________ Strike Water Temp: ________°

Starting Mash Temp: ________° Final Mash Temp: ________°

Sparge Water Amount: ________ Sparge Water Temp: ________°

Sparge Temp: ________°

Pre-boil Gravity: ________

Notes: ____

____

For Extract Batches

Water Volume: ________

Grains Steeped for: ________ minutes at ________°

Extract(s) Added: ❑ Start of Boil ❑ ________ Minutes into Boil

Step 2: Boil

Hops & Other Ingredients Schedule

	Time
1. ________________________________	________
2. ________________________________	________
3. ________________________________	________
4. ________________________________	________
5. ________________________________	________
6. ________________________________	________

Step 3: Chilling and Pitching

Chill Method: ❑ Ice Bath ❑ Immersion Coil ❑ ________

Chill Start Time: ________

Chill Finish Time: ________

Original Gravity: ________

Wort Temp at Pitching: ________°

Wort Volume: ________

Aeration Method: ❑ Agitation ❑ Forced

Notes: ____

FERMENTATION

Primary Start Date/Time: ____________________

❑ Glass Carboy ❑ Plastic Bucket ❑ ____________

❑ Airlock ❑ Blow-off Tube ❑ ____________

Date/Time: ____________ Temp: ______°

Date/Time: ____________ Temp: ______°

Date/Time: ____________ Temp: ______°

Date/Time: ____________ Temp: ______°

Date/Time: ____________ Temp: ______°

Date/Time: ____________ Temp: ______°

Date/Time: ____________ Temp: ______°

Date/Time: ____________ Temp: ______°

Additions to Primary or Secondary: ____________

Secondary Start Date/Time: ____________________

Date/Time: ____________ Temp: ______°

Date/Time: ____________ Temp: ______°

Date/Time: ____________ Temp: ______°

Date/Time: ____________ Temp: ______°

Date/Time: ____________ Temp: ______°

Date/Time: ____________ Temp: ______°

Date/Time: ____________ Temp: ______°

Date/Time: ____________ Temp: ______°

Notes: ____________

PACKAGING

Date/Time: ____________

Final Gravity: ____________

(_____ OG – _____ FG) × 131 = _____% ABV

❑ Bottle ❑ Keg

Priming Agent: ____________

Amount: ____________

-or-

CO_2 Setting: ________ psi for _____ days

Sanitizing Agent/Method: ____________

STORAGE/AGING

Date/Time: ________ Temp: ______°

Date/Time: ________ Temp: ______°

Date/Time: ________ Temp: ______°

Date/Time: ________ Temp: ______°

Date/Time: ________ Temp: ______°

Date/Time: ________ Temp: ______°

Notes: ____________

FIRST TASTING

Date/Time: ______________________

Tasters: ______________________

Glassware: ______________________

Serving Temp: __________°

Appearance: ______________________

Aroma: ______________________

Flavor: ______________________

Finish: ______________________

FINAL THOUGHTS

BEER INFO

Beer Name: ______________________

____

Style: ______________________

Brewer(s): ______________________

____

❑ Partial Mash/Extract ❑ All-Grain

Preliminary Notes and Expectations

Gallons: ______________________

OG/FG: ______________________

ABV: ______________________

IBU: ______________________

SRM: ______________________

BREWING DAY

Date: ______________________

Start Time: ______________________

Beer(s) Imbibed: ______________________

____

____

____

____

____

Soundtrack: ______________________

____

____

____

____

____

INGREDIENTS

Grain Bill & Fermentables

	Amount	Cost
1.		
2.		
3.		
4.		
5.		
6.		
7.		
8.		

Hop Bill

	Amount	AA%	Cost
1.			
2.			
3.			
4.			
5.			
6.			

Other Ingredients

	Amount	Cost
1.		
2.		
3.		

Yeast

Variety: ______________________ Cost: __________

Water Adjustments

Notes: ______________________

Total Cost: __________

BREWING

Step 1: Mash

❑ Single-Infusion ❑ Step-Infusion ❑ Decoction

Strike Water Amount: ______ Strike Water Temp: ______°

Starting Mash Temp: ______° Final Mash Temp: ______°

Sparge Water Amount: ______ Sparge Water Temp: ______°

Sparge Temp: ______°

Pre-boil Gravity: ______

Notes: ______

For Extract Batches

Water Volume: ______

Grains Steeped for: ______ minutes at ______°

Extract(s) Added: ❑ Start of Boil ❑ ______ Minutes into Boil

Step 2: Boil

Hops & Other Ingredients Schedule

	Time
1. ______	______
2. ______	______
3. ______	______
4. ______	______
5. ______	______
6. ______	______

Step 3: Chilling and Pitching

Chill Method: ❑ Ice Bath ❑ Immersion Coil ❑ ______

Chill Start Time: ______

Chill Finish Time: ______

Original Gravity: ______

Wort Temp at Pitching: ______°

Wort Volume: ______

Aeration Method: ❑ Agitation ❑ Forced

Notes: ______

FERMENTATION

Primary Start Date/Time: ______

❑ Glass Carboy ❑ Plastic Bucket ❑ ______

❑ Airlock ❑ Blow-off Tube ❑ ______

Date/Time: ______ Temp: ______°

Date/Time: ______ Temp: ______°

Date/Time: ______ Temp: ______°

Date/Time: ______ Temp: ______°

Date/Time: ______ Temp: ______°

Date/Time: ______ Temp: ______°

Date/Time: ______ Temp: ______°

Date/Time: ______ Temp: ______°

Additions to Primary or Secondary: ______

Secondary Start Date/Time: ______

Date/Time: ______ Temp: ______°

Date/Time: ______ Temp: ______°

Date/Time: ______ Temp: ______°

Date/Time: ______ Temp: ______°

Date/Time: ______ Temp: ______°

Date/Time: ______ Temp: ______°

Date/Time: ______ Temp: ______°

Date/Time: ______ Temp: ______°

Notes: ______

PACKAGING

Date/Time: ______

Final Gravity: ______

(______ OG – ______ FG) × 131 = ______% ABV

❑ Bottle ❑ Keg

Priming Agent: ______

Amount: ______

-or-

CO_2 Setting: ______ psi for ______ days

Sanitizing Agent/Method: ______

STORAGE/AGING

Date/Time: ______ Temp: ______°

Date/Time: ______ Temp: ______°

Date/Time: ______ Temp: ______°

Date/Time: ______ Temp: ______°

Date/Time: ______ Temp: ______°

Date/Time: ______ Temp: ______°

Notes: ______

FIRST TASTING

Date/Time: ____________________

Tasters: ____________________

Glassware: ____________________

Serving Temp: ________°

Appearance: ____________________

Aroma: ____________________

Flavor: ____________________

Finish: ____________________

FINAL THOUGHTS

BEER INFO

Beer Name: ____________________

____

Style: ____________________

Brewer(s): ____________________

____

❑ Partial Mash/Extract ❑ All-Grain

Preliminary Notes and Expectations

Gallons: ____________________

OG/FG: ____________________

ABV: ____________________

IBU: ____________________

SRM: ____________________

BREWING DAY

Date: ____________________

Start Time: ____________________

Beer(s) Imbibed: ____________________

____

____

____

____

____

Soundtrack: ____________________

____

____

____

____

____

INGREDIENTS

Grain Bill & Fermentables

	Amount	Cost
1.		
2.		
3.		
4.		
5.		
6.		
7.		
8.		

Hop Bill

	Amount	AA%	Cost
1.			
2.			
3.			
4.			
5.			
6.			

Other Ingredients

	Amount	Cost
1.		
2.		
3.		

Yeast

Variety: ____________________ Cost: __________

Water Adjustments

Notes: ____________________

Total Cost: __________

BREWING

Step 1: Mash

❑ Single-Infusion ❑ Step-Infusion ❑ Decoction

Strike Water Amount: ________ Strike Water Temp: ________°

Starting Mash Temp: ________° Final Mash Temp: ________°

Sparge Water Amount: ________ Sparge Water Temp: ________°

Sparge Temp: ________°

Pre-boil Gravity: ________

Notes: ____

____

For Extract Batches

Water Volume: ________

Grains Steeped for: ________ minutes at ________°

Extract(s) Added: ❑ Start of Boil ❑ ________ Minutes into Boil

Step 2: Boil

Hops & Other Ingredients Schedule

		Time
1.	____________________	________
2.	____________________	________
3.	____________________	________
4.	____________________	________
5.	____________________	________
6.	____________________	________

Step 3: Chilling and Pitching

Chill Method: ❑ Ice Bath ❑ Immersion Coil ❑ ________

Chill Start Time: ________

Chill Finish Time: ________

Original Gravity: ________

Wort Temp at Pitching: ________°

Wort Volume: ________

Aeration Method: ❑ Agitation ❑ Forced

Notes: ____

FERMENTATION

Primary Start Date/Time: ______

❑ Glass Carboy ❑ Plastic Bucket ❑ ______

❑ Airlock ❑ Blow-off Tube ❑ ______

Date/Time: ______ Temp: ______°

Date/Time: ______ Temp: ______°

Date/Time: ______ Temp: ______°

Date/Time: ______ Temp: ______°

Date/Time: ______ Temp: ______°

Date/Time: ______ Temp: ______°

Date/Time: ______ Temp: ______°

Date/Time: ______ Temp: ______°

Additions to Primary or Secondary: ______

______

______

______

______

Secondary Start Date/Time: ______

Date/Time: ______ Temp: ______°

Date/Time: ______ Temp: ______°

Date/Time: ______ Temp: ______°

Date/Time: ______ Temp: ______°

Date/Time: ______ Temp: ______°

Date/Time: ______ Temp: ______°

Date/Time: ______ Temp: ______°

Date/Time: ______ Temp: ______°

Notes: ______

______

______

______

______

PACKAGING

Date/Time: ______

Final Gravity: ______

(______ OG – ______ FG) × 131 = ______% ABV

❑ Bottle ❑ Keg

Priming Agent: ______

Amount: ______

-or-

CO_2 Setting: ______ psi for ______ days

Sanitizing Agent/Method: ______

______

______

STORAGE/AGING

Date/Time: ______ Temp: ______°

Date/Time: ______ Temp: ______°

Date/Time: ______ Temp: ______°

Date/Time: ______ Temp: ______°

Date/Time: ______ Temp: ______°

Date/Time: ______ Temp: ______°

Notes: ______

______

______

______

______

______

______

______

______

______

FIRST TASTING

Date/Time: __________

Tasters: __________

Glassware: __________

Serving Temp: __________°

Appearance: __________

Aroma: __________

Flavor: __________

Finish: __________

FINAL THOUGHTS

BEER INFO

Beer Name: ______________________

____

Style: ______________________

Brewer(s): ______________________

____

❑ Partial Mash/Extract ❑ All-Grain

Preliminary Notes and Expectations

Gallons: ______________________

OG/FG: ______________________

ABV: ______________________

IBU: ______________________

SRM: ______________________

BREWING DAY

Date: ______________________

Start Time: ______________________

Beer(s) Imbibed: ______________________

____

____

____

____

____

Soundtrack: ______________________

____

____

____

____

____

INGREDIENTS

Grain Bill & Fermentables

	Amount	Cost
1.		
2.		
3.		
4.		
5.		
6.		
7.		
8.		

Hop Bill

	Amount	AA%	Cost
1.			
2.			
3.			
4.			
5.			
6.			

Other Ingredients

	Amount	Cost
1.		
2.		
3.		

Yeast

Variety: ______________________ Cost: __________

Water Adjustments

Notes: ______________________

Total Cost: __________

BREWING

Step 1: Mash

❑ Single-Infusion ❑ Step-Infusion ❑ Decoction

Strike Water Amount: ________ Strike Water Temp: ________°

Starting Mash Temp: ________° Final Mash Temp: ________°

Sparge Water Amount: ________ Sparge Water Temp: ________°

Sparge Temp: ________°

Pre-boil Gravity: ________

Notes: ____

____

For Extract Batches

Water Volume: ________

Grains Steeped for: ________ minutes at ________°

Extract(s) Added: ❑ Start of Boil ❑ ________ Minutes into Boil

Step 2: Boil

Hops & Other Ingredients Schedule

		Time
1.	________________________________	________
2.	________________________________	________
3.	________________________________	________
4.	________________________________	________
5.	________________________________	________
6.	________________________________	________

Step 3: Chilling and Pitching

Chill Method: ❑ Ice Bath ❑ Immersion Coil ❑ ________

Chill Start Time: ________

Chill Finish Time: ________

Original Gravity: ________

Wort Temp at Pitching: ________°

Wort Volume: ________

Aeration Method: ❑ Agitation ❑ Forced

Notes: ____

FERMENTATION

Primary Start Date/Time: ______________________

❑ Glass Carboy ❑ Plastic Bucket ❑ ____________

❑ Airlock ❑ Blow-off Tube ❑ ____________

Date/Time: ______________________ Temp: ________°

Date/Time: ______________________ Temp: ________°

Date/Time: ______________________ Temp: ________°

Date/Time: ______________________ Temp: ________°

Date/Time: ______________________ Temp: ________°

Date/Time: ______________________ Temp: ________°

Date/Time: ______________________ Temp: ________°

Date/Time: ______________________ Temp: ________°

Additions to Primary or Secondary: ______________________

____

____

____

____

Secondary Start Date/Time: ______________________

Date/Time: ______________________ Temp: ________°

Date/Time: ______________________ Temp: ________°

Date/Time: ______________________ Temp: ________°

Date/Time: ______________________ Temp: ________°

Date/Time: ______________________ Temp: ________°

Date/Time: ______________________ Temp: ________°

Date/Time: ______________________ Temp: ________°

Date/Time: ______________________ Temp: ________°

Notes: ______________________

____

____

____

____

PACKAGING

Date/Time: ______________________

Final Gravity: ______________________

(_____ OG – _____ FG) × 131 = _____% ABV

❑ Bottle ❑ Keg

Priming Agent: ______________________

Amount: ______________________

-or-

CO_2 Setting: ________ psi for _____ days

Sanitizing Agent/Method: ______________________

____

____

STORAGE/AGING

Date/Time: ________ Temp: ________°

Date/Time: ________ Temp: ________°

Date/Time: ________ Temp: ________°

Date/Time: ________ Temp: ________°

Date/Time: ________ Temp: ________°

Date/Time: ________ Temp: ________°

Notes: ______________________

____

____

____

____

____

____

____

____

____

FIRST TASTING

Date/Time: ____________________

Tasters: ____________________

Glassware: ____________________

Serving Temp: ________°

Appearance: ____________________

Aroma: ____________________

Flavor: ____________________

Finish: ____________________

FINAL THOUGHTS

BEER INFO

Beer Name: ______________________

____

Style: ______________________

Brewer(s): ______________________

____

❑ Partial Mash/Extract ❑ All-Grain

Preliminary Notes and Expectations

Gallons: ______________________

OG/FG: ______________________

ABV: ______________________

IBU: ______________________

SRM: ______________________

BREWING DAY

Date: ______________________

Start Time: ______________________

Beer(s) Imbibed: ______________________

____

____

____

____

____

Soundtrack: ______________________

____

____

____

____

____

INGREDIENTS

Grain Bill & Fermentables

	Amount	Cost
1.		
2.		
3.		
4.		
5.		
6.		
7.		
8.		

Hop Bill

	Amount	AA%	Cost
1.			
2.			
3.			
4.			
5.			
6.			

Other Ingredients

	Amount	Cost
1.		
2.		
3.		

Yeast

Variety: ______________________ Cost: ________

Water Adjustments

Notes: ______________________

Total Cost: ________

BREWING

Step 1: Mash

❑ Single-Infusion ❑ Step-Infusion ❑ Decoction

Strike Water Amount: __________ Strike Water Temp: __________°

Starting Mash Temp: __________° Final Mash Temp: __________°

Sparge Water Amount: __________ Sparge Water Temp: __________°

Sparge Temp: __________°

Pre-boil Gravity: __________

Notes: ____

____

For Extract Batches

Water Volume: __________

Grains Steeped for: __________ minutes at __________°

Extract(s) Added: ❑ Start of Boil ❑ __________ Minutes into Boil

Step 2: Boil

Hops & Other Ingredients Schedule

	Time
1. ____________________	__________
2. ____________________	__________
3. ____________________	__________
4. ____________________	__________
5. ____________________	__________
6. ____________________	__________

Step 3: Chilling and Pitching

Chill Method: ❑ Ice Bath ❑ Immersion Coil ❑ __________

Chill Start Time: __________

Chill Finish Time: __________

Original Gravity: __________

Wort Temp at Pitching: __________°

Wort Volume: __________

Aeration Method: ❑ Agitation ❑ Forced

Notes: ____

FERMENTATION

Primary Start Date/Time: ______

❑ Glass Carboy ❑ Plastic Bucket ❑ ______

❑ Airlock ❑ Blow-off Tube ❑ ______

Date/Time: ______ Temp: ______°

Date/Time: ______ Temp: ______°

Date/Time: ______ Temp: ______°

Date/Time: ______ Temp: ______°

Date/Time: ______ Temp: ______°

Date/Time: ______ Temp: ______°

Date/Time: ______ Temp: ______°

Date/Time: ______ Temp: ______°

Additions to Primary or Secondary: ______

Secondary Start Date/Time: ______

Date/Time: ______ Temp: ______°

Date/Time: ______ Temp: ______°

Date/Time: ______ Temp: ______°

Date/Time: ______ Temp: ______°

Date/Time: ______ Temp: ______°

Date/Time: ______ Temp: ______°

Date/Time: ______ Temp: ______°

Date/Time: ______ Temp: ______°

Notes: ______

PACKAGING

Date/Time: ______

Final Gravity: ______

(____ OG – ____ FG) × 131 = ____% ABV

❑ Bottle ❑ Keg

Priming Agent: ______

Amount: ______

-or-

CO_2 Setting: ______ psi for ____ days

Sanitizing Agent/Method: ______

STORAGE/AGING

Date/Time: ______ Temp: ______°

Date/Time: ______ Temp: ______°

Date/Time: ______ Temp: ______°

Date/Time: ______ Temp: ______°

Date/Time: ______ Temp: ______°

Date/Time: ______ Temp: ______°

Notes: ______

FIRST TASTING

Date/Time: ______

Tasters: ______

Glassware: ______

Serving Temp: ______°

Appearance: ______

Aroma: ______

Flavor: ______

Finish: ______

FINAL THOUGHTS

BEER INFO

Beer Name: ______________________

____

Style: ______________________

Brewer(s): ______________________

____

❑ Partial Mash/Extract ❑ All-Grain

Preliminary Notes and Expectations

Gallons: ______________________

OG/FG: ______________________

ABV: ______________________

IBU: ______________________

SRM: ______________________

BREWING DAY

Date: ______________________

Start Time: ______________________

Beer(s) Imbibed: ______________________

____

____

____

____

____

Soundtrack: ______________________

____

____

____

____

____

INGREDIENTS

Grain Bill & Fermentables

	Amount	Cost
1.		
2.		
3.		
4.		
5.		
6.		
7.		
8.		

Hop Bill

	Amount	AA%	Cost
1.			
2.			
3.			
4.			
5.			
6.			

Other Ingredients

	Amount	Cost
1.		
2.		
3.		

Yeast

Variety: ______________________ Cost: ________

Water Adjustments

Notes: ______________________

Total Cost: ________

BREWING

Step 1: Mash

❑ Single-Infusion ❑ Step-Infusion ❑ Decoction

Strike Water Amount: __________ Strike Water Temp: __________°

Starting Mash Temp: __________° Final Mash Temp: __________°

Sparge Water Amount: __________ Sparge Water Temp: __________°

Sparge Temp: __________°

Pre-boil Gravity: __________

Notes: ______________________________

____

For Extract Batches

Water Volume: __________

Grains Steeped for: __________ minutes at __________°

Extract(s) Added: ❑ Start of Boil ❑ __________ Minutes into Boil

Step 2: Boil

Hops & Other Ingredients Schedule

	Time
1. ______________________________	__________
2. ______________________________	__________
3. ______________________________	__________
4. ______________________________	__________
5. ______________________________	__________
6. ______________________________	__________

Step 3: Chilling and Pitching

Chill Method: ❑ Ice Bath ❑ Immersion Coil ❑ __________

Chill Start Time: __________

Chill Finish Time: __________

Original Gravity: __________

Wort Temp at Pitching: __________°

Wort Volume: __________

Aeration Method: ❑ Agitation ❑ Forced

Notes: ______________________________

FERMENTATION

Primary Start Date/Time: ______

❑ Glass Carboy ❑ Plastic Bucket ❑ ______

❑ Airlock ❑ Blow-off Tube ❑ ______

Date/Time: ______ Temp: ______°

Date/Time: ______ Temp: ______°

Date/Time: ______ Temp: ______°

Date/Time: ______ Temp: ______°

Date/Time: ______ Temp: ______°

Date/Time: ______ Temp: ______°

Date/Time: ______ Temp: ______°

Date/Time: ______ Temp: ______°

Additions to Primary or Secondary: ______

Secondary Start Date/Time: ______

Date/Time: ______ Temp: ______°

Date/Time: ______ Temp: ______°

Date/Time: ______ Temp: ______°

Date/Time: ______ Temp: ______°

Date/Time: ______ Temp: ______°

Date/Time: ______ Temp: ______°

Date/Time: ______ Temp: ______°

Date/Time: ______ Temp: ______°

Notes: ______

PACKAGING

Date/Time: ______

Final Gravity: ______

(____ OG – ____ FG) × 131 = ____% ABV

❑ Bottle ❑ Keg

Priming Agent: ______

Amount: ______

-or-

CO_2 Setting: ______ psi for ____ days

Sanitizing Agent/Method: ______

STORAGE/AGING

Date/Time: ______ Temp: ______°

Date/Time: ______ Temp: ______°

Date/Time: ______ Temp: ______°

Date/Time: ______ Temp: ______°

Date/Time: ______ Temp: ______°

Date/Time: ______ Temp: ______°

Notes: ______

FIRST TASTING

Date/Time: ______

Tasters: ______

Glassware: ______

Serving Temp: ______°

Appearance: ______

Aroma: ______

Flavor: ______

Finish: ______

FINAL THOUGHTS

BEER INFO

Beer Name: ____________________

____

Style: ____________________

Brewer(s): ____________________

____

❑ Partial Mash/Extract ❑ All-Grain

Preliminary Notes and Expectations

Gallons: ____________________

OG/FG: ____________________

ABV: ____________________

IBU: ____________________

SRM: ____________________

BREWING DAY

Date: ____________________

Start Time: ____________________

Beer(s) Imbibed: ____________________

____

____

____

____

____

Soundtrack: ____________________

____

____

____

____

____

INGREDIENTS

Grain Bill & Fermentables

	Amount	Cost
1.		
2.		
3.		
4.		
5.		
6.		
7.		
8.		

Hop Bill

	Amount	AA%	Cost
1.			
2.			
3.			
4.			
5.			
6.			

Other Ingredients

	Amount	Cost
1.		
2.		
3.		

Yeast

Variety: ____________________ Cost: __________

Water Adjustments

Notes: ____________________

Total Cost: __________

BREWING

Step 1: Mash

❑ Single-Infusion ❑ Step-Infusion ❑ Decoction

Strike Water Amount: ________ Strike Water Temp: ________°

Starting Mash Temp: ________° Final Mash Temp: ________°

Sparge Water Amount: ________ Sparge Water Temp: ________°

Sparge Temp: ________°

Pre-boil Gravity: ________

Notes: ____

____

For Extract Batches

Water Volume: ________

Grains Steeped for: ________ minutes at ________°

Extract(s) Added: ❑ Start of Boil ❑ ________ Minutes into Boil

Step 2: Boil

Hops & Other Ingredients Schedule

	Time
1. ____	________
2. ____	________
3. ____	________
4. ____	________
5. ____	________
6. ____	________

Step 3: Chilling and Pitching

Chill Method: ❑ Ice Bath ❑ Immersion Coil ❑ ________

Chill Start Time: ________

Chill Finish Time: ________

Original Gravity: ________

Wort Temp at Pitching: ________°

Wort Volume: ________

Aeration Method: ❑ Agitation ❑ Forced

Notes: ____

FERMENTATION

Primary Start Date/Time: ____________________

❑ Glass Carboy ❑ Plastic Bucket ❑ ____________

❑ Airlock ❑ Blow-off Tube ❑ ____________

Date/Time: ____________ Temp: ______°

Date/Time: ____________ Temp: ______°

Date/Time: ____________ Temp: ______°

Date/Time: ____________ Temp: ______°

Date/Time: ____________ Temp: ______°

Date/Time: ____________ Temp: ______°

Date/Time: ____________ Temp: ______°

Date/Time: ____________ Temp: ______°

Additions to Primary or Secondary: ____________________

Secondary Start Date/Time: ____________________

Date/Time: ____________ Temp: ______°

Date/Time: ____________ Temp: ______°

Date/Time: ____________ Temp: ______°

Date/Time: ____________ Temp: ______°

Date/Time: ____________ Temp: ______°

Date/Time: ____________ Temp: ______°

Date/Time: ____________ Temp: ______°

Date/Time: ____________ Temp: ______°

Notes: ____________________

PACKAGING

Date/Time: ____________________

Final Gravity: ____________________

(_____ OG – _____ FG) × 131 = _____% ABV

❑ Bottle ❑ Keg

Priming Agent: ____________________

Amount: ____________________

-or-

CO_2 Setting: __________ psi for _____ days

Sanitizing Agent/Method: ____________________

STORAGE/AGING

Date/Time: __________ Temp: ______°

Date/Time: __________ Temp: ______°

Date/Time: __________ Temp: ______°

Date/Time: __________ Temp: ______°

Date/Time: __________ Temp: ______°

Date/Time: __________ Temp: ______°

Notes: ____________________

FIRST TASTING

Date/Time: ______________________

Tasters: ______________________

Glassware: ______________________

Serving Temp: __________°

Appearance: ______________________

Aroma: ______________________

Flavor: ______________________

Finish: ______________________

FINAL THOUGHTS

BEER INFO

Beer Name: ______________________

____

Style: ______________________

Brewer(s): ______________________

____

❑ Partial Mash/Extract ❑ All-Grain

Preliminary Notes and Expectations

Gallons: ______________________

OG/FG: ______________________

ABV: ______________________

IBU: ______________________

SRM: ______________________

BREWING DAY

Date: ______________________

Start Time: ______________________

Beer(s) Imbibed: ______________________

____

____

____

____

____

Soundtrack: ______________________

____

____

____

____

____

INGREDIENTS

Grain Bill & Fermentables

	Amount	Cost
1.		
2.		
3.		
4.		
5.		
6.		
7.		
8.		

Hop Bill

	Amount	AA%	Cost
1.			
2.			
3.			
4.			
5.			
6.			

Other Ingredients

	Amount	Cost
1.		
2.		
3.		

Yeast

Variety: ______________________ Cost: ________

Water Adjustments

Notes: ______________________

Total Cost: ________

BREWING

Step 1: Mash

❑ Single-Infusion ❑ Step-Infusion ❑ Decoction

Strike Water Amount: ________ Strike Water Temp: ________°

Starting Mash Temp: ________° Final Mash Temp: ________°

Sparge Water Amount: ________ Sparge Water Temp: ________°

Sparge Temp: ________°

Pre-boil Gravity: ________

Notes: ____

____

For Extract Batches

Water Volume: ________

Grains Steeped for: ________ minutes at ________°

Extract(s) Added: ❑ Start of Boil ❑ ________ Minutes into Boil

Step 2: Boil

Hops & Other Ingredients Schedule

	Time
1. ________________	________
2. ________________	________
3. ________________	________
4. ________________	________
5. ________________	________
6. ________________	________

Step 3: Chilling and Pitching

Chill Method: ❑ Ice Bath ❑ Immersion Coil ❑ ________

Chill Start Time: ________

Chill Finish Time: ________

Original Gravity: ________

Wort Temp at Pitching: ________°

Wort Volume: ________

Aeration Method: ❑ Agitation ❑ Forced

Notes: ____

FERMENTATION

Primary Start Date/Time: ______

❑ Glass Carboy ❑ Plastic Bucket ❑ ______

❑ Airlock ❑ Blow-off Tube ❑ ______

Date/Time: ______ Temp: ______°

Date/Time: ______ Temp: ______°

Date/Time: ______ Temp: ______°

Date/Time: ______ Temp: ______°

Date/Time: ______ Temp: ______°

Date/Time: ______ Temp: ______°

Date/Time: ______ Temp: ______°

Date/Time: ______ Temp: ______°

Additions to Primary or Secondary: ______

______

______

______

______

Secondary Start Date/Time: ______

Date/Time: ______ Temp: ______°

Date/Time: ______ Temp: ______°

Date/Time: ______ Temp: ______°

Date/Time: ______ Temp: ______°

Date/Time: ______ Temp: ______°

Date/Time: ______ Temp: ______°

Date/Time: ______ Temp: ______°

Date/Time: ______ Temp: ______°

Notes: ______

______

______

______

______

PACKAGING

Date/Time: ______

Final Gravity: ______

(______ OG – ______ FG) × 131 = ______% ABV

❑ Bottle ❑ Keg

Priming Agent: ______

Amount: ______

-or-

CO_2 Setting: ______ psi for ______ days

Sanitizing Agent/Method: ______

______

______

STORAGE/AGING

Date/Time: ______ Temp: ______°

Date/Time: ______ Temp: ______°

Date/Time: ______ Temp: ______°

Date/Time: ______ Temp: ______°

Date/Time: ______ Temp: ______°

Date/Time: ______ Temp: ______°

Notes: ______

______

______

______

______

______

______

______

______

______

FIRST TASTING

Date/Time: ____

Tasters: ____

Glassware: ____

Serving Temp: __________°

Appearance: ____

Aroma: ____

Flavor: ____

Finish: ____

FINAL THOUGHTS

BEER INFO

Beer Name: ____________________

____

Style: ____________________

Brewer(s): ____________________

____

❑ Partial Mash/Extract ❑ All-Grain

Preliminary Notes and Expectations

Gallons: ____________________

OG/FG: ____________________

ABV: ____________________

IBU: ____________________

SRM: ____________________

BREWING DAY

Date: ____________________

Start Time: ____________________

Beer(s) Imbibed: ____________________

____

____

____

____

____

Soundtrack: ____________________

____

____

____

____

____

INGREDIENTS

Grain Bill & Fermentables

	Amount	Cost
1.		
2.		
3.		
4.		
5.		
6.		
7.		
8.		

Hop Bill

	Amount	AA%	Cost
1.			
2.			
3.			
4.			
5.			
6.			

Other Ingredients

	Amount	Cost
1.		
2.		
3.		

Yeast

Variety: ____________________ Cost: __________

Water Adjustments

Notes: ____________________

Total Cost: __________

Step 1: Mash

❑ Single-Infusion ❑ Step-Infusion ❑ Decoction

Strike Water Amount: ________ Strike Water Temp: ________°

Starting Mash Temp: ________° Final Mash Temp: ________°

Sparge Water Amount: ________ Sparge Water Temp: ________°

Sparge Temp: ________°

Pre-boil Gravity: ________

Notes: ____

____

For Extract Batches

Water Volume: ________

Grains Steeped for: ________ minutes at ________°

Extract(s) Added: ❑ Start of Boil ❑ ________ Minutes into Boil

Step 2: Boil

Hops & Other Ingredients Schedule

	Time
1. ________________________________	________
2. ________________________________	________
3. ________________________________	________
4. ________________________________	________
5. ________________________________	________
6. ________________________________	________

Step 3: Chilling and Pitching

Chill Method: ❑ Ice Bath ❑ Immersion Coil ❑ ________

Chill Start Time: ________

Chill Finish Time: ________

Original Gravity: ________

Wort Temp at Pitching: ________°

Wort Volume: ________

Aeration Method: ❑ Agitation ❑ Forced

Notes: ____

FERMENTATION

Primary Start Date/Time: ______

❑ Glass Carboy ❑ Plastic Bucket ❑ ______

❑ Airlock ❑ Blow-off Tube ❑ ______

Date/Time: ______ Temp: ______°

Date/Time: ______ Temp: ______°

Date/Time: ______ Temp: ______°

Date/Time: ______ Temp: ______°

Date/Time: ______ Temp: ______°

Date/Time: ______ Temp: ______°

Date/Time: ______ Temp: ______°

Date/Time: ______ Temp: ______°

Additions to Primary or Secondary: ______

______

______

______

______

Secondary Start Date/Time: ______

Date/Time: ______ Temp: ______°

Date/Time: ______ Temp: ______°

Date/Time: ______ Temp: ______°

Date/Time: ______ Temp: ______°

Date/Time: ______ Temp: ______°

Date/Time: ______ Temp: ______°

Date/Time: ______ Temp: ______°

Date/Time: ______ Temp: ______°

Notes: ______

______

______

______

______

PACKAGING

Date/Time: ______

Final Gravity: ______

(______ OG – ______ FG) × 131 = ______% ABV

❑ Bottle ❑ Keg

Priming Agent: ______

Amount: ______

-or-

CO_2 Setting: ______ psi for ______ days

Sanitizing Agent/Method: ______

______

______

STORAGE/AGING

Date/Time: ______ Temp: ______°

Date/Time: ______ Temp: ______°

Date/Time: ______ Temp: ______°

Date/Time: ______ Temp: ______°

Date/Time: ______ Temp: ______°

Date/Time: ______ Temp: ______°

Notes: ______

______

______

______

______

______

______

______

______

______

FIRST TASTING

Date/Time: ______

Tasters: ______

Glassware: ______

Serving Temp: ______°

Appearance: ______

Aroma: ______

Flavor: ______

Finish: ______

FINAL THOUGHTS

BEER INFO

Beer Name: ______________________

____

Style: ______________________

Brewer(s): ______________________

____

❑ Partial Mash/Extract ❑ All-Grain

Preliminary Notes and Expectations

Gallons: ______________________

OG/FG: ______________________

ABV: ______________________

IBU: ______________________

SRM: ______________________

BREWING DAY

Date: ______________________

Start Time: ______________________

Beer(s) Imbibed: ______________________

____

____

____

____

____

Soundtrack: ______________________

____

____

____

____

____

INGREDIENTS

Grain Bill & Fermentables

	Amount	Cost
1.		
2.		
3.		
4.		
5.		
6.		
7.		
8.		

Hop Bill

	Amount	AA%	Cost
1.			
2.			
3.			
4.			
5.			
6.			

Other Ingredients

	Amount	Cost
1.		
2.		
3.		

Yeast

Variety: ______________________ Cost: __________

Water Adjustments

Notes: ______________________

Total Cost: __________

BREWING

Step 1: Mash

❑ Single-Infusion ❑ Step-Infusion ❑ Decoction

Strike Water Amount: ________ Strike Water Temp: ________°

Starting Mash Temp: ________° Final Mash Temp: ________°

Sparge Water Amount: ________ Sparge Water Temp: ________°

Sparge Temp: ________°

Pre-boil Gravity: ________

Notes: ____

____

For Extract Batches

Water Volume: ________

Grains Steeped for: ________ minutes at ________°

Extract(s) Added: ❑ Start of Boil ❑ ________ Minutes into Boil

Step 2: Boil

Hops & Other Ingredients Schedule

	Time
1. ________________________________	________
2. ________________________________	________
3. ________________________________	________
4. ________________________________	________
5. ________________________________	________
6. ________________________________	________

Step 3: Chilling and Pitching

Chill Method: ❑ Ice Bath ❑ Immersion Coil ❑ ________

Chill Start Time: ________

Chill Finish Time: ________

Original Gravity: ________

Wort Temp at Pitching: ________°

Wort Volume: ________

Aeration Method: ❑ Agitation ❑ Forced

Notes: ____

FERMENTATION

Primary Start Date/Time: ______

❑ Glass Carboy ❑ Plastic Bucket ❑ ______

❑ Airlock ❑ Blow-off Tube ❑ ______

Date/Time: ______ Temp: ______°

Date/Time: ______ Temp: ______°

Date/Time: ______ Temp: ______°

Date/Time: ______ Temp: ______°

Date/Time: ______ Temp: ______°

Date/Time: ______ Temp: ______°

Date/Time: ______ Temp: ______°

Date/Time: ______ Temp: ______°

Additions to Primary or Secondary: ______

Secondary Start Date/Time: ______

Date/Time: ______ Temp: ______°

Date/Time: ______ Temp: ______°

Date/Time: ______ Temp: ______°

Date/Time: ______ Temp: ______°

Date/Time: ______ Temp: ______°

Date/Time: ______ Temp: ______°

Date/Time: ______ Temp: ______°

Date/Time: ______ Temp: ______°

Notes: ______

PACKAGING

Date/Time: ______

Final Gravity: ______

(______ OG – ______ FG) × 131 = ______% ABV

❑ Bottle ❑ Keg

Priming Agent: ______

Amount: ______

-or-

CO_2 Setting: ______ psi for ______ days

Sanitizing Agent/Method: ______

STORAGE/AGING

Date/Time: ______ Temp: ______°

Date/Time: ______ Temp: ______°

Date/Time: ______ Temp: ______°

Date/Time: ______ Temp: ______°

Date/Time: ______ Temp: ______°

Date/Time: ______ Temp: ______°

Notes: ______

FIRST TASTING

Date/Time: ____________________

Tasters: ____________________

Glassware: ____________________

Serving Temp: __________°

Appearance: ____________________

Aroma: ____________________

Flavor: ____________________

Finish: ____________________

FINAL THOUGHTS

BEER INFO

Beer Name: ______________________

____

Style: ______________________

Brewer(s): ______________________

____

❑ Partial Mash/Extract ❑ All-Grain

Preliminary Notes and Expectations

Gallons: ______________________

OG/FG: ______________________

ABV: ______________________

IBU: ______________________

SRM: ______________________

BREWING DAY

Date: ______________________

Start Time: ______________________

Beer(s) Imbibed: ______________________

____

____

____

____

____

Soundtrack: ______________________

____

____

____

____

____

INGREDIENTS

Grain Bill & Fermentables

	Amount	Cost
1.		
2.		
3.		
4.		
5.		
6.		
7.		
8.		

Hop Bill

	Amount	AA%	Cost
1.			
2.			
3.			
4.			
5.			
6.			

Other Ingredients

	Amount	Cost
1.		
2.		
3.		

Yeast

Variety: ______________________ Cost: __________

Water Adjustments

Notes: ______________________

Total Cost: __________

BREWING

Step 1: Mash

❑ Single-Infusion ❑ Step-Infusion ❑ Decoction

Strike Water Amount: __________ Strike Water Temp: __________°

Starting Mash Temp: __________° Final Mash Temp: __________°

Sparge Water Amount: __________ Sparge Water Temp: __________°

Sparge Temp: __________°

Pre-boil Gravity: __________

Notes: ____

____

For Extract Batches

Water Volume: __________

Grains Steeped for: __________ minutes at __________°

Extract(s) Added: ❑ Start of Boil ❑ __________ Minutes into Boil

Step 2: Boil

Hops & Other Ingredients Schedule

	Time
1. ______________________________	________
2. ______________________________	________
3. ______________________________	________
4. ______________________________	________
5. ______________________________	________
6. ______________________________	________

Step 3: Chilling and Pitching

Chill Method: ❑ Ice Bath ❑ Immersion Coil ❑ __________

Chill Start Time: __________

Chill Finish Time: __________

Original Gravity: __________

Wort Temp at Pitching: __________°

Wort Volume: __________

Aeration Method: ❑ Agitation ❑ Forced

Notes: ____

FERMENTATION

Primary Start Date/Time: ______

❑ Glass Carboy ❑ Plastic Bucket ❑ ______

❑ Airlock ❑ Blow-off Tube ❑ ______

Date/Time: ______ Temp: ______°

Date/Time: ______ Temp: ______°

Date/Time: ______ Temp: ______°

Date/Time: ______ Temp: ______°

Date/Time: ______ Temp: ______°

Date/Time: ______ Temp: ______°

Date/Time: ______ Temp: ______°

Date/Time: ______ Temp: ______°

Additions to Primary or Secondary: ______

Secondary Start Date/Time: ______

Date/Time: ______ Temp: ______°

Date/Time: ______ Temp: ______°

Date/Time: ______ Temp: ______°

Date/Time: ______ Temp: ______°

Date/Time: ______ Temp: ______°

Date/Time: ______ Temp: ______°

Date/Time: ______ Temp: ______°

Date/Time: ______ Temp: ______°

Notes: ______

PACKAGING

Date/Time: ______

Final Gravity: ______

(____ OG – ____ FG) × 131 = ____% ABV

❑ Bottle ❑ Keg

Priming Agent: ______

Amount: ______

-or-

CO_2 Setting: ______ psi for ____ days

Sanitizing Agent/Method: ______

STORAGE/AGING

Date/Time: ______ Temp: ______°

Date/Time: ______ Temp: ______°

Date/Time: ______ Temp: ______°

Date/Time: ______ Temp: ______°

Date/Time: ______ Temp: ______°

Date/Time: ______ Temp: ______°

Notes: ______

FIRST TASTING

Date/Time: ______________________

Tasters: ______________________

Glassware: ______________________

Serving Temp: ________°

Appearance: ______________________

Aroma: ______________________

Flavor: ______________________

Finish: ______________________

FINAL THOUGHTS

BEER INFO

Beer Name: ____________________

____

Style: ____________________

Brewer(s): ____________________

____

❑ Partial Mash/Extract ❑ All-Grain

Preliminary Notes and Expectations

Gallons: ____________________

OG/FG: ____________________

ABV: ____________________

IBU: ____________________

SRM: ____________________

BREWING DAY

Date: ____________________

Start Time: ____________________

Beer(s) Imbibed: ____________________

____

____

____

____

____

Soundtrack: ____________________

____

____

____

____

____

INGREDIENTS

Grain Bill & Fermentables

	Amount	Cost
1.		
2.		
3.		
4.		
5.		
6.		
7.		
8.		

Hop Bill

	Amount	AA%	Cost
1.			
2.			
3.			
4.			
5.			
6.			

Other Ingredients

	Amount	Cost
1.		
2.		
3.		

Yeast

Variety: ____________________ Cost: ________

Water Adjustments

Notes: ____________________

Total Cost: ________

BREWING

Step 1: Mash

❑ Single-Infusion ❑ Step-Infusion ❑ Decoction

Strike Water Amount: ________ Strike Water Temp: ________°

Starting Mash Temp: ________° Final Mash Temp: ________°

Sparge Water Amount: ________ Sparge Water Temp: ________°

Sparge Temp: ________°

Pre-boil Gravity: ________

Notes: ____

____

For Extract Batches

Water Volume: ________

Grains Steeped for: ________ minutes at ________°

Extract(s) Added: ❑ Start of Boil ❑ ________ Minutes into Boil

Step 2: Boil

Hops & Other Ingredients Schedule

	Time
1. ________________________________	________
2. ________________________________	________
3. ________________________________	________
4. ________________________________	________
5. ________________________________	________
6. ________________________________	________

Step 3: Chilling and Pitching

Chill Method: ❑ Ice Bath ❑ Immersion Coil ❑ ________

Chill Start Time: ________

Chill Finish Time: ________

Original Gravity: ________

Wort Temp at Pitching: ________°

Wort Volume: ________

Aeration Method: ❑ Agitation ❑ Forced

Notes: ____

FERMENTATION

Primary Start Date/Time: ____________________

❏ Glass Carboy ❏ Plastic Bucket ❏ ____________

❏ Airlock ❏ Blow-off Tube ❏ ____________

Date/Time: ____________________ Temp: ________°

Date/Time: ____________________ Temp: ________°

Date/Time: ____________________ Temp: ________°

Date/Time: ____________________ Temp: ________°

Date/Time: ____________________ Temp: ________°

Date/Time: ____________________ Temp: ________°

Date/Time: ____________________ Temp: ________°

Date/Time: ____________________ Temp: ________°

Additions to Primary or Secondary: ____________________

Secondary Start Date/Time: ____________________

Date/Time: ____________________ Temp: ________°

Date/Time: ____________________ Temp: ________°

Date/Time: ____________________ Temp: ________°

Date/Time: ____________________ Temp: ________°

Date/Time: ____________________ Temp: ________°

Date/Time: ____________________ Temp: ________°

Date/Time: ____________________ Temp: ________°

Date/Time: ____________________ Temp: ________°

Notes: ____________________

PACKAGING

Date/Time: ____________________

Final Gravity: ____________________

(_____ OG – _____ FG) × 131 = _____% ABV

❏ Bottle ❏ Keg

Priming Agent: ____________________

Amount: ____________________

-or-

CO_2 Setting: __________ psi for _____ days

Sanitizing Agent/Method: ____________________

STORAGE/AGING

Date/Time: __________ Temp: ________°

Date/Time: __________ Temp: ________°

Date/Time: __________ Temp: ________°

Date/Time: __________ Temp: ________°

Date/Time: __________ Temp: ________°

Date/Time: __________ Temp: ________°

Notes: ____________________

FIRST TASTING

Date/Time: ____________________

Tasters: ____________________

Glassware: ____________________

Serving Temp: ________°

Appearance: ____________________

Aroma: ____________________

Flavor: ____________________

Finish: ____________________

FINAL THOUGHTS

BEER INFO

Beer Name: ____________

____

Style: ____________

Brewer(s): ____________

____

❑ Partial Mash/Extract ❑ All-Grain

Preliminary Notes and Expectations

Gallons: ____________

OG/FG: ____________

ABV: ____________

IBU: ____________

SRM: ____________

BREWING DAY

Date: ____________

Start Time: ____________

Beer(s) Imbibed: ____________

____

____

____

____

____

Soundtrack: ____________

____

____

____

____

____

INGREDIENTS

Grain Bill & Fermentables

	Amount	Cost
1.		
2.		
3.		
4.		
5.		
6.		
7.		
8.		

Hop Bill

	Amount	AA%	Cost
1.			
2.			
3.			
4.			
5.			
6.			

Other Ingredients

	Amount	Cost
1.		
2.		
3.		

Yeast

Variety: ____________ Cost: ____________

Water Adjustments

Notes: ____________

Total Cost: ____________

BREWING

Step 1: Mash

❑ Single-Infusion ❑ Step-Infusion ❑ Decoction

Strike Water Amount: ________ Strike Water Temp: ________°

Starting Mash Temp: ________° Final Mash Temp: ________°

Sparge Water Amount: ________ Sparge Water Temp: ________°

Sparge Temp: ________°

Pre-boil Gravity: ________

Notes: ____

____

For Extract Batches

Water Volume: ________

Grains Steeped for: ________ minutes at ________°

Extract(s) Added: ❑ Start of Boil ❑ ________ Minutes into Boil

Step 2: Boil

Hops & Other Ingredients Schedule

	Time
1. ________________________	________
2. ________________________	________
3. ________________________	________
4. ________________________	________
5. ________________________	________
6. ________________________	________

Step 3: Chilling and Pitching

Chill Method: ❑ Ice Bath ❑ Immersion Coil ❑ ________

Chill Start Time: ________

Chill Finish Time: ________

Original Gravity: ________

Wort Temp at Pitching: ________°

Wort Volume: ________

Aeration Method: ❑ Agitation ❑ Forced

Notes: ____

FERMENTATION

Primary Start Date/Time: ____________________

❑ Glass Carboy ❑ Plastic Bucket ❑ ____________

❑ Airlock ❑ Blow-off Tube ❑ ____________

Date/Time: ____________________ Temp: ________°

Date/Time: ____________________ Temp: ________°

Date/Time: ____________________ Temp: ________°

Date/Time: ____________________ Temp: ________°

Date/Time: ____________________ Temp: ________°

Date/Time: ____________________ Temp: ________°

Date/Time: ____________________ Temp: ________°

Date/Time: ____________________ Temp: ________°

Additions to Primary or Secondary: ____________________

Secondary Start Date/Time: ____________________

Date/Time: ____________________ Temp: ________°

Date/Time: ____________________ Temp: ________°

Date/Time: ____________________ Temp: ________°

Date/Time: ____________________ Temp: ________°

Date/Time: ____________________ Temp: ________°

Date/Time: ____________________ Temp: ________°

Date/Time: ____________________ Temp: ________°

Date/Time: ____________________ Temp: ________°

Notes: ____________________

PACKAGING

Date/Time: ____________________

Final Gravity: ____________________

(_____ OG – _____ FG) × 131 = _____% ABV

❑ Bottle ❑ Keg

Priming Agent: ____________________

Amount: ____________________

-or-

CO_2 Setting: ________ psi for _____ days

Sanitizing Agent/Method: ____________________

STORAGE/AGING

Date/Time: ________ Temp: ________°

Date/Time: ________ Temp: ________°

Date/Time: ________ Temp: ________°

Date/Time: ________ Temp: ________°

Date/Time: ________ Temp: ________°

Date/Time: ________ Temp: ________°

Notes: ____________________

FIRST TASTING

Date/Time: ______

Tasters: ______

Glassware: ______

Serving Temp: ______°

Appearance: ______

Aroma: ______

Flavor: ______

Finish: ______

FINAL THOUGHTS

BEER INFO

Beer Name: ______________________

____

Style: ______________________

Brewer(s): ______________________

____

❑ Partial Mash/Extract ❑ All-Grain

Preliminary Notes and Expectations

Gallons: ______________________

OG/FG: ______________________

ABV: ______________________

IBU: ______________________

SRM: ______________________

BREWING DAY

Date: ______________________

Start Time: ______________________

Beer(s) Imbibed: ______________________

____

____

____

____

____

Soundtrack: ______________________

____

____

____

____

____

INGREDIENTS

Grain Bill & Fermentables

	Amount	Cost
1.		
2.		
3.		
4.		
5.		
6.		
7.		
8.		

Hop Bill

	Amount	AA%	Cost
1.			
2.			
3.			
4.			
5.			
6.			

Other Ingredients

	Amount	Cost
1.		
2.		
3.		

Yeast

Variety: ______________________ Cost: ________

Water Adjustments

Notes: ______________________

Total Cost: ________

BREWING

Step 1: Mash

❑ Single-Infusion ❑ Step-Infusion ❑ Decoction

Strike Water Amount: __________ Strike Water Temp: __________°

Starting Mash Temp: __________° Final Mash Temp: __________°

Sparge Water Amount: __________ Sparge Water Temp: __________°

Sparge Temp: __________°

Pre-boil Gravity: __________

Notes: ______________________________

____

For Extract Batches

Water Volume: __________

Grains Steeped for: __________ minutes at __________°

Extract(s) Added: ❑ Start of Boil ❑ __________ Minutes into Boil

Step 2: Boil

Hops & Other Ingredients Schedule

	Time
1. ______________________________	__________
2. ______________________________	__________
3. ______________________________	__________
4. ______________________________	__________
5. ______________________________	__________
6. ______________________________	__________

Step 3: Chilling and Pitching

Chill Method: ❑ Ice Bath ❑ Immersion Coil ❑ __________

Chill Start Time: __________

Chill Finish Time: __________

Original Gravity: __________

Wort Temp at Pitching: __________°

Wort Volume: __________

Aeration Method: ❑ Agitation ❑ Forced

Notes: ______________________________

FERMENTATION

Primary Start Date/Time: ____________________

❑ Glass Carboy ❑ Plastic Bucket ❑ ____________

❑ Airlock ❑ Blow-off Tube ❑ ____________

Date/Time: ____________ Temp: ______°

Date/Time: ____________ Temp: ______°

Date/Time: ____________ Temp: ______°

Date/Time: ____________ Temp: ______°

Date/Time: ____________ Temp: ______°

Date/Time: ____________ Temp: ______°

Date/Time: ____________ Temp: ______°

Date/Time: ____________ Temp: ______°

Additions to Primary or Secondary: ____________________

Secondary Start Date/Time: ____________________

Date/Time: ____________ Temp: ______°

Date/Time: ____________ Temp: ______°

Date/Time: ____________ Temp: ______°

Date/Time: ____________ Temp: ______°

Date/Time: ____________ Temp: ______°

Date/Time: ____________ Temp: ______°

Date/Time: ____________ Temp: ______°

Date/Time: ____________ Temp: ______°

Notes: ____________________

PACKAGING

Date/Time: ____________________

Final Gravity: ____________________

(_____ OG – _____ FG) × 131 = _____% ABV

❑ Bottle ❑ Keg

Priming Agent: ____________________

Amount: ____________________

-or-

CO_2 Setting: ________ psi for _____ days

Sanitizing Agent/Method: ____________________

STORAGE/AGING

Date/Time: ________ Temp: ______°

Date/Time: ________ Temp: ______°

Date/Time: ________ Temp: ______°

Date/Time: ________ Temp: ______°

Date/Time: ________ Temp: ______°

Date/Time: ________ Temp: ______°

Notes: ____________________

FIRST TASTING

Date/Time: ______

Tasters: ______

Glassware: ______

Serving Temp: ______°

Appearance: ______

Aroma: ______

Flavor: ______

Finish: ______

FINAL THOUGHTS

BEER INFO

Beer Name: ______________________

____

Style: ______________________

Brewer(s): ______________________

____

❑ Partial Mash/Extract ❑ All-Grain

Preliminary Notes and Expectations

Gallons: ______________________

OG/FG: ______________________

ABV: ______________________

IBU: ______________________

SRM: ______________________

BREWING DAY

Date: ______________________

Start Time: ______________________

Beer(s) Imbibed: ______________________

____

____

____

____

____

Soundtrack: ______________________

____

____

____

____

____

INGREDIENTS

Grain Bill & Fermentables

	Amount	Cost
1.		
2.		
3.		
4.		
5.		
6.		
7.		
8.		

Hop Bill

	Amount	AA%	Cost
1.			
2.			
3.			
4.			
5.			
6.			

Other Ingredients

	Amount	Cost
1.		
2.		
3.		

Yeast

Variety: ______________________ Cost: __________

Water Adjustments

Notes: ______________________

Total Cost: __________

BREWING

Step 1: Mash

❑ Single-Infusion ❑ Step-Infusion ❑ Decoction

Strike Water Amount: ________ Strike Water Temp: ________°

Starting Mash Temp: ________° Final Mash Temp: ________°

Sparge Water Amount: ________ Sparge Water Temp: ________°

Sparge Temp: ________°

Pre-boil Gravity: ________

Notes: ____

____

For Extract Batches

Water Volume: ________

Grains Steeped for: ________ minutes at ________°

Extract(s) Added: ❑ Start of Boil ❑ ________ Minutes into Boil

Step 2: Boil

Hops & Other Ingredients Schedule

	Time
1. ________________________________	________
2. ________________________________	________
3. ________________________________	________
4. ________________________________	________
5. ________________________________	________
6. ________________________________	________

Step 3: Chilling and Pitching

Chill Method: ❑ Ice Bath ❑ Immersion Coil ❑ ________

Chill Start Time: ________

Chill Finish Time: ________

Original Gravity: ________

Wort Temp at Pitching: ________°

Wort Volume: ________

Aeration Method: ❑ Agitation ❑ Forced

Notes: ________________________________

FERMENTATION

Primary Start Date/Time: ______________________

❑ Glass Carboy ❑ Plastic Bucket ❑ ____________

❑ Airlock ❑ Blow-off Tube ❑ ____________

Date/Time: ______________ Temp: ______°

Date/Time: ______________ Temp: ______°

Date/Time: ______________ Temp: ______°

Date/Time: ______________ Temp: ______°

Date/Time: ______________ Temp: ______°

Date/Time: ______________ Temp: ______°

Date/Time: ______________ Temp: ______°

Date/Time: ______________ Temp: ______°

Additions to Primary or Secondary: ______________________

Secondary Start Date/Time: ______________________

Date/Time: ______________ Temp: ______°

Date/Time: ______________ Temp: ______°

Date/Time: ______________ Temp: ______°

Date/Time: ______________ Temp: ______°

Date/Time: ______________ Temp: ______°

Date/Time: ______________ Temp: ______°

Date/Time: ______________ Temp: ______°

Date/Time: ______________ Temp: ______°

Notes: ______________________

PACKAGING

Date/Time: ______________________

Final Gravity: ______________________

(_____ OG – _____ FG) × 131 = _____% ABV

❑ Bottle ❑ Keg

Priming Agent: ______________________

Amount: ______________________

-or-

CO_2 Setting: __________ psi for _____ days

Sanitizing Agent/Method: ______________________

STORAGE/AGING

Date/Time: __________ Temp: ______°

Date/Time: __________ Temp: ______°

Date/Time: __________ Temp: ______°

Date/Time: __________ Temp: ______°

Date/Time: __________ Temp: ______°

Date/Time: __________ Temp: ______°

Notes: ______________________

FIRST TASTING

Date/Time: ______

Tasters: ______

Glassware: ______

Serving Temp: ______°

Appearance: ______

Aroma: ______

Flavor: ______

Finish: ______

FINAL THOUGHTS

BEER INFO

Beer Name: ______________________

____

Style: ______________________

Brewer(s): ______________________

____

❑ Partial Mash/Extract ❑ All-Grain

Preliminary Notes and Expectations

Gallons: ______________________

OG/FG: ______________________

ABV: ______________________

IBU: ______________________

SRM: ______________________

BREWING DAY

Date: ______________________

Start Time: ______________________

Beer(s) Imbibed: ______________________

____

____

____

____

____

Soundtrack: ______________________

____

____

____

____

____

INGREDIENTS

Grain Bill & Fermentables

	Amount	Cost
1.		
2.		
3.		
4.		
5.		
6.		
7.		
8.		

Hop Bill

	Amount	AA%	Cost
1.			
2.			
3.			
4.			
5.			
6.			

Other Ingredients

	Amount	Cost
1.		
2.		
3.		

Yeast

Variety: ______________________ Cost: __________

Water Adjustments

Notes: ______________________

Total Cost: __________

BREWING

Step 1: Mash

❑ Single-Infusion ❑ Step-Infusion ❑ Decoction

Strike Water Amount: ________ Strike Water Temp: ________°

Starting Mash Temp: ________° Final Mash Temp: ________°

Sparge Water Amount: ________ Sparge Water Temp: ________°

Sparge Temp: ________°

Pre-boil Gravity: ________

Notes: ____

____

For Extract Batches

Water Volume: ________

Grains Steeped for: ________ minutes at ________°

Extract(s) Added: ❑ Start of Boil ❑ ________ Minutes into Boil

Step 2: Boil

Hops & Other Ingredients Schedule

	Time
1. ________________________________	________
2. ________________________________	________
3. ________________________________	________
4. ________________________________	________
5. ________________________________	________
6. ________________________________	________

Step 3: Chilling and Pitching

Chill Method: ❑ Ice Bath ❑ Immersion Coil ❑ ________

Chill Start Time: ________

Chill Finish Time: ________

Original Gravity: ________

Wort Temp at Pitching: ________°

Wort Volume: ________

Aeration Method: ❑ Agitation ❑ Forced

Notes: ____

FERMENTATION

Primary Start Date/Time: ______________________

❑ Glass Carboy ❑ Plastic Bucket ❑ ______________

❑ Airlock ❑ Blow-off Tube ❑ ______________

Date/Time: ______________________ Temp: ________°

Date/Time: ______________________ Temp: ________°

Date/Time: ______________________ Temp: ________°

Date/Time: ______________________ Temp: ________°

Date/Time: ______________________ Temp: ________°

Date/Time: ______________________ Temp: ________°

Date/Time: ______________________ Temp: ________°

Date/Time: ______________________ Temp: ________°

Additions to Primary or Secondary: ______________________

____

____

____

____

Secondary Start Date/Time: ______________________

Date/Time: ______________________ Temp: ________°

Date/Time: ______________________ Temp: ________°

Date/Time: ______________________ Temp: ________°

Date/Time: ______________________ Temp: ________°

Date/Time: ______________________ Temp: ________°

Date/Time: ______________________ Temp: ________°

Date/Time: ______________________ Temp: ________°

Date/Time: ______________________ Temp: ________°

Notes: ______________________________________

____

____

____

____

PACKAGING

Date/Time: ______________________

Final Gravity: ______________________

(_____ OG – _____ FG) × 131 = _____% ABV

❑ Bottle ❑ Keg

Priming Agent: ______________________

Amount: ______________________

-or-

CO_2 Setting: __________ psi for _____ days

Sanitizing Agent/Method: ______________

____

____

STORAGE/AGING

Date/Time: __________ Temp: ________°

Date/Time: __________ Temp: ________°

Date/Time: __________ Temp: ________°

Date/Time: __________ Temp: ________°

Date/Time: __________ Temp: ________°

Date/Time: __________ Temp: ________°

Notes: ______________________________

____

____

____

____

____

____

____

____

____

FIRST TASTING

Date/Time: ___

Tasters: ___

Glassware: ___

Serving Temp: ___°

Appearance: ___

Aroma: ___

Flavor: ___

Finish: ___

FINAL THOUGHTS

BEER INFO

Beer Name: ______________________

____

Style: ______________________

Brewer(s): ______________________

____

❑ Partial Mash/Extract ❑ All-Grain

Preliminary Notes and Expectations

Gallons: ______________________

OG/FG: ______________________

ABV: ______________________

IBU: ______________________

SRM: ______________________

BREWING DAY

Date: ______________________

Start Time: ______________________

Beer(s) Imbibed: ______________________

____

____

____

____

____

Soundtrack: ______________________

____

____

____

____

____

INGREDIENTS

Grain Bill & Fermentables

	Amount	Cost
1.		
2.		
3.		
4.		
5.		
6.		
7.		
8.		

Hop Bill

	Amount	AA%	Cost
1.			
2.			
3.			
4.			
5.			
6.			

Other Ingredients

	Amount	Cost
1.		
2.		
3.		

Yeast

Variety: ______________________ Cost: __________

Water Adjustments

Notes: ______________________

Total Cost: __________

Step 1: Mash

❑ Single-Infusion ❑ Step-Infusion ❑ Decoction

Strike Water Amount: __________ Strike Water Temp: __________°

Starting Mash Temp: __________° Final Mash Temp: __________°

Sparge Water Amount: __________ Sparge Water Temp: __________°

Sparge Temp: __________°

Pre-boil Gravity: __________

Notes: ____

____

For Extract Batches

Water Volume: __________

Grains Steeped for: __________ minutes at __________°

Extract(s) Added: ❑ Start of Boil ❑ __________ Minutes into Boil

Step 2: Boil

Hops & Other Ingredients Schedule

	Time
1. ______________________________	________
2. ______________________________	________
3. ______________________________	________
4. ______________________________	________
5. ______________________________	________
6. ______________________________	________

Step 3: Chilling and Pitching

Chill Method: ❑ Ice Bath ❑ Immersion Coil ❑ __________

Chill Start Time: __________

Chill Finish Time: __________

Original Gravity: __________

Wort Temp at Pitching: __________°

Wort Volume: __________

Aeration Method: ❑ Agitation ❑ Forced

Notes: ______________________________

FERMENTATION

Primary Start Date/Time: ______

❑ Glass Carboy ❑ Plastic Bucket ❑ ______

❑ Airlock ❑ Blow-off Tube ❑ ______

Date/Time: ______ Temp: ______°

Date/Time: ______ Temp: ______°

Date/Time: ______ Temp: ______°

Date/Time: ______ Temp: ______°

Date/Time: ______ Temp: ______°

Date/Time: ______ Temp: ______°

Date/Time: ______ Temp: ______°

Date/Time: ______ Temp: ______°

Additions to Primary or Secondary: ______

Secondary Start Date/Time: ______

Date/Time: ______ Temp: ______°

Date/Time: ______ Temp: ______°

Date/Time: ______ Temp: ______°

Date/Time: ______ Temp: ______°

Date/Time: ______ Temp: ______°

Date/Time: ______ Temp: ______°

Date/Time: ______ Temp: ______°

Date/Time: ______ Temp: ______°

Notes: ______

PACKAGING

Date/Time: ______

Final Gravity: ______

(______ OG – ______ FG) × 131 = ______% ABV

❑ Bottle ❑ Keg

Priming Agent: ______

Amount: ______

-or-

CO_2 Setting: ______ psi for ______ days

Sanitizing Agent/Method: ______

STORAGE/AGING

Date/Time: ______ Temp: ______°

Date/Time: ______ Temp: ______°

Date/Time: ______ Temp: ______°

Date/Time: ______ Temp: ______°

Date/Time: ______ Temp: ______°

Date/Time: ______ Temp: ______°

Notes: ______

FIRST TASTING

Date/Time: ____________________

Tasters: ____________________

Glassware: ____________________

Serving Temp: ________°

Appearance: ____________________

Aroma: ____________________

Flavor: ____________________

Finish: ____________________

FINAL THOUGHTS

BEER INFO

Beer Name: ______________________

____

Style: ______________________

Brewer(s): ______________________

____

❑ Partial Mash/Extract ❑ All-Grain

Preliminary Notes and Expectations

Gallons: ______________________

OG/FG: ______________________

ABV: ______________________

IBU: ______________________

SRM: ______________________

BREWING DAY

Date: ______________________

Start Time: ______________________

Beer(s) Imbibed: ______________________

____

____

____

____

____

Soundtrack: ______________________

____

____

____

____

____

INGREDIENTS

Grain Bill & Fermentables

	Amount	Cost
1.		
2.		
3.		
4.		
5.		
6.		
7.		
8.		

Hop Bill

	Amount	AA%	Cost
1.			
2.			
3.			
4.			
5.			
6.			

Other Ingredients

	Amount	Cost
1.		
2.		
3.		

Yeast

Variety: ______________________ Cost: ________

Water Adjustments

Notes: ______________________

Total Cost: ________

BREWING

Step 1: Mash

❑ Single-Infusion ❑ Step-Infusion ❑ Decoction

Strike Water Amount: __________ Strike Water Temp: __________°

Starting Mash Temp: __________° Final Mash Temp: __________°

Sparge Water Amount: __________ Sparge Water Temp: __________°

Sparge Temp: __________°

Pre-boil Gravity: __________

Notes: ____

____

For Extract Batches

Water Volume: __________

Grains Steeped for: __________ minutes at __________°

Extract(s) Added: ❑ Start of Boil ❑ __________ Minutes into Boil

Step 2: Boil

Hops & Other Ingredients Schedule

	Time
1. ______________________________	__________
2. ______________________________	__________
3. ______________________________	__________
4. ______________________________	__________
5. ______________________________	__________
6. ______________________________	__________

Step 3: Chilling and Pitching

Chill Method: ❑ Ice Bath ❑ Immersion Coil ❑ __________

Chill Start Time: __________

Chill Finish Time: __________

Original Gravity: __________

Wort Temp at Pitching: __________°

Wort Volume: __________

Aeration Method: ❑ Agitation ❑ Forced

Notes: ______________________________

FERMENTATION

Primary Start Date/Time: ____________________

❑ Glass Carboy ❑ Plastic Bucket ❑ ____________

❑ Airlock ❑ Blow-off Tube ❑ ____________

Date/Time: ____________ Temp: ______°

Date/Time: ____________ Temp: ______°

Date/Time: ____________ Temp: ______°

Date/Time: ____________ Temp: ______°

Date/Time: ____________ Temp: ______°

Date/Time: ____________ Temp: ______°

Date/Time: ____________ Temp: ______°

Date/Time: ____________ Temp: ______°

Additions to Primary or Secondary: ____________________

Secondary Start Date/Time: ____________________

Date/Time: ____________ Temp: ______°

Date/Time: ____________ Temp: ______°

Date/Time: ____________ Temp: ______°

Date/Time: ____________ Temp: ______°

Date/Time: ____________ Temp: ______°

Date/Time: ____________ Temp: ______°

Date/Time: ____________ Temp: ______°

Date/Time: ____________ Temp: ______°

Notes: ____________________

PACKAGING

Date/Time: ____________

Final Gravity: ____________

(____ OG – ____ FG) × 131 = ____% ABV

❑ Bottle ❑ Keg

Priming Agent: ____________

Amount: ____________

-or-

CO_2 Setting: ________ psi for ____ days

Sanitizing Agent/Method: ____________

STORAGE/AGING

Date/Time: ________ Temp: ______°

Date/Time: ________ Temp: ______°

Date/Time: ________ Temp: ______°

Date/Time: ________ Temp: ______°

Date/Time: ________ Temp: ______°

Date/Time: ________ Temp: ______°

Notes: ____________________

FIRST TASTING

Date/Time: ______

Tasters: ______

Glassware: ______

Serving Temp: ______°

Appearance: ______

Aroma: ______

Flavor: ______

Finish: ______

FINAL THOUGHTS

BEER INFO

Beer Name: ______________________

____

Style: ______________________

Brewer(s): ______________________

____

❑ Partial Mash/Extract ❑ All-Grain

Preliminary Notes and Expectations

Gallons: ______________________

OG/FG: ______________________

ABV: ______________________

IBU: ______________________

SRM: ______________________

BREWING DAY

Date: ______________________

Start Time: ______________________

Beer(s) Imbibed: ______________________

____

____

____

____

____

Soundtrack: ______________________

____

____

____

____

____

INGREDIENTS

Grain Bill & Fermentables

	Amount	Cost
1.		
2.		
3.		
4.		
5.		
6.		
7.		
8.		

Hop Bill

	Amount	AA%	Cost
1.			
2.			
3.			
4.			
5.			
6.			

Other Ingredients

	Amount	Cost
1.		
2.		
3.		

Yeast

Variety: ______________________ Cost: __________

Water Adjustments

Notes: ______________________

Total Cost: __________

BREWING

Step 1: Mash

❑ Single-Infusion ❑ Step-Infusion ❑ Decoction

Strike Water Amount: ________ Strike Water Temp: ________°

Starting Mash Temp: ________° Final Mash Temp: ________°

Sparge Water Amount: ________ Sparge Water Temp: ________°

Sparge Temp: ________°

Pre-boil Gravity: ________

Notes: ____

____

For Extract Batches

Water Volume: ________

Grains Steeped for: ________ minutes at ________°

Extract(s) Added: ❑ Start of Boil ❑ ________ Minutes into Boil

Step 2: Boil

Hops & Other Ingredients Schedule

	Time
1. ________________________________	________
2. ________________________________	________
3. ________________________________	________
4. ________________________________	________
5. ________________________________	________
6. ________________________________	________

Step 3: Chilling and Pitching

Chill Method: ❑ Ice Bath ❑ Immersion Coil ❑ ________

Chill Start Time: ________

Chill Finish Time: ________

Original Gravity: ________

Wort Temp at Pitching: ________°

Wort Volume: ________

Aeration Method: ❑ Agitation ❑ Forced

Notes: ____

FERMENTATION

Primary Start Date/Time: ____________________

❑ Glass Carboy ❑ Plastic Bucket ❑ ____________

❑ Airlock ❑ Blow-off Tube ❑ ____________

Date/Time: ____________________ Temp: ________°

Date/Time: ____________________ Temp: ________°

Date/Time: ____________________ Temp: ________°

Date/Time: ____________________ Temp: ________°

Date/Time: ____________________ Temp: ________°

Date/Time: ____________________ Temp: ________°

Date/Time: ____________________ Temp: ________°

Date/Time: ____________________ Temp: ________°

Additions to Primary or Secondary: ____________________

Secondary Start Date/Time: ____________________

Date/Time: ____________________ Temp: ________°

Date/Time: ____________________ Temp: ________°

Date/Time: ____________________ Temp: ________°

Date/Time: ____________________ Temp: ________°

Date/Time: ____________________ Temp: ________°

Date/Time: ____________________ Temp: ________°

Date/Time: ____________________ Temp: ________°

Date/Time: ____________________ Temp: ________°

Notes: ____________________

PACKAGING

Date/Time: ____________________

Final Gravity: ____________________

(_____ OG – _____ FG) × 131 = _____% ABV

❑ Bottle ❑ Keg

Priming Agent: ____________________

Amount: ____________________

-or-

CO_2 Setting: ________ psi for _____ days

Sanitizing Agent/Method: ____________________

STORAGE/AGING

Date/Time: ________ Temp: ________°

Date/Time: ________ Temp: ________°

Date/Time: ________ Temp: ________°

Date/Time: ________ Temp: ________°

Date/Time: ________ Temp: ________°

Date/Time: ________ Temp: ________°

Notes: ____________________

FIRST TASTING

Date/Time: ______

Tasters: ______

Glassware: ______

Serving Temp: ______°

Appearance: ______

Aroma: ______

Flavor: ______

Finish: ______

FINAL THOUGHTS

BEER INFO

Beer Name: ______________________

____

Style: ______________________

Brewer(s): ______________________

____

❑ Partial Mash/Extract ❑ All-Grain

Preliminary Notes and Expectations

Gallons: ______________________

OG/FG: ______________________

ABV: ______________________

IBU: ______________________

SRM: ______________________

BREWING DAY

Date: ______________________

Start Time: ______________________

Beer(s) Imbibed: ______________________

____

____

____

____

____

Soundtrack: ______________________

____

____

____

____

____

INGREDIENTS

Grain Bill & Fermentables

	Amount	Cost
1.		
2.		
3.		
4.		
5.		
6.		
7.		
8.		

Hop Bill

	Amount	AA%	Cost
1.			
2.			
3.			
4.			
5.			
6.			

Other Ingredients

	Amount	Cost
1.		
2.		
3.		

Yeast

Variety: ______________________ Cost: __________

Water Adjustments

Notes: ______________________

Total Cost: __________

BREWING

Step 1: Mash

❑ Single-Infusion ❑ Step-Infusion ❑ Decoction

Strike Water Amount: ________ Strike Water Temp: ________°

Starting Mash Temp: ________° Final Mash Temp: ________°

Sparge Water Amount: ________ Sparge Water Temp: ________°

Sparge Temp: ________°

Pre-boil Gravity: ________

Notes: ____

____

For Extract Batches

Water Volume: ________

Grains Steeped for: ________ minutes at ________°

Extract(s) Added: ❑ Start of Boil ❑ ________ Minutes into Boil

Step 2: Boil

Hops & Other Ingredients Schedule

	Time
1. ________________________________	________
2. ________________________________	________
3. ________________________________	________
4. ________________________________	________
5. ________________________________	________
6. ________________________________	________

Step 3: Chilling and Pitching

Chill Method: ❑ Ice Bath ❑ Immersion Coil ❑ ________

Chill Start Time: ________

Chill Finish Time: ________

Original Gravity: ________

Wort Temp at Pitching: ________°

Wort Volume: ________

Aeration Method: ❑ Agitation ❑ Forced

Notes: ____

FERMENTATION

Primary Start Date/Time: ____________

❑ Glass Carboy ❑ Plastic Bucket ❑ ____________

❑ Airlock ❑ Blow-off Tube ❑ ____________

Date/Time: ____________ Temp: ______°

Date/Time: ____________ Temp: ______°

Date/Time: ____________ Temp: ______°

Date/Time: ____________ Temp: ______°

Date/Time: ____________ Temp: ______°

Date/Time: ____________ Temp: ______°

Date/Time: ____________ Temp: ______°

Date/Time: ____________ Temp: ______°

Additions to Primary or Secondary: ____________

Secondary Start Date/Time: ____________

Date/Time: ____________ Temp: ______°

Date/Time: ____________ Temp: ______°

Date/Time: ____________ Temp: ______°

Date/Time: ____________ Temp: ______°

Date/Time: ____________ Temp: ______°

Date/Time: ____________ Temp: ______°

Date/Time: ____________ Temp: ______°

Date/Time: ____________ Temp: ______°

Notes: ____________

PACKAGING

Date/Time: ____________

Final Gravity: ____________

(______ OG – ______ FG) × 131 = ______% ABV

❑ Bottle ❑ Keg

Priming Agent: ____________

Amount: ____________

-or-

CO_2 Setting: ______ psi for ______ days

Sanitizing Agent/Method: ____________

STORAGE/AGING

Date/Time: ______ Temp: ______°

Date/Time: ______ Temp: ______°

Date/Time: ______ Temp: ______°

Date/Time: ______ Temp: ______°

Date/Time: ______ Temp: ______°

Date/Time: ______ Temp: ______°

Notes: ____________

FIRST TASTING

Date/Time: ______

Tasters: ______

Glassware: ______

Serving Temp: ______°

Appearance: ______

Aroma: ______

Flavor: ______

Finish: ______

FINAL THOUGHTS

FURTHER RESOURCES

Magazines

All About Beer www.allaboutbeer.com

BeerAdvocate www.beeradvocate.com

Brew Your Own www.byo.com

Zymurgy www.homebrewersassociation.org/pages/zymurgy/current-issue

Books

Calagione, Sam. *Extreme Brewing: A Deluxe Edition with 14 New Homebrew Recipes.* Quarry Books: Beverly, MA, 2012.

Daniels, Ray. *Designing Great Beers: The Ultimate Guide to Brewing Classic Beer Styles.* Brewers Publications: Denver, CO, 2000.

Hieronymus, Stan. *For the Love of Hops: The Practical Guide to Aroma, Bitterness and the Culture of Hops.* Brewers Publications: Denver, CO, 2013.

Koch, Greg, and Matt Allyn. *The Brewer's Apprentice: An Insider's Guide to the Art and Craft of Beer Brewing, Taught by the Masters.* Quarry Books: Beverly, MA, 2012.

Kunath, Brian. *The Brewer's Bible: How to Brew Delicious Beers at Home.* Chartwell Books: New York, NY, 2011.

Palmer, John. *How to Brew: Everything You Need to Know to Brew Beer Right the First Time.* Brewers Publications: Denver, CO, 2006.

Palmer, John and Jamil Zainasheff. *Brewing Classic Styles: 80 Winning Recipes Anyone Can Brew.* Brewers Publications: Denver, CO, 2007.

Papazian, Charlie. *The Complete Joy of Homebrewing, Third Edition.* Harper: New York, NY, 2003.

———. *The Homebrewer's Companion.* Harper: New York, NY, 2003.

Pattinson, Ronald. *The Home Brewer's Guide to Vintage Beers.* Quarry Books, Beverly, MA, 2013.

Strong, Gordon. *Brewing Better Beer: Master Lessons for Advanced Homebrewers.* Brewers Publications: Denver, CO, 2011.

White, Chris and Jamil Zainasheff. *Yeast: The Practical Guide to Beer Fermentation.* Brewers Publications: Denver, CO, 2010.

Retailers

BrewGadgets.com – 866-591-8247; www.brewgadgets.com

Home Brew Mart – 800-581-2739; www.homebrewmart.com

Homebrew Heaven – 425-355-8865; www.homebrewheaven.com

HomeBrew USA – 888-459-BREW; www.homebrewusa.com

Keystone Homebrew Supply – 215-855-0100; www.keystonehomebrew.com

Love2Brew – 888-654-5511; www.love2brew.com

Midwest Homebrewing and Winemaking Supplies – 888-449-2739; www.midwestsupplies.com

Monster Brew – 800-454-0274; www.monsterbrew.com

MoreBeer! – 800-600-0033; www.morebeer.com

Northern Brewer Homebrew Supply – 800-681-2739; www.northernbrewer.com

GLOSSARY OF BEER TERMS

ABV—Alcohol by volume, the measurement of the alcohol content in beer expressed as a percentage of the total volume.

ABW—Alcohol by weight, the measurement of the alcohol content in beer expressed as a percentage of the total weight.

acetic acid—A vinegary off flavor produced by a bacteria that's acceptable in certain sour and wood-aged beers.

adjunct—Any nonenzymatic fermentable sugar. Adjuncts include syrups, refined sugars, and unmalted cereals such as flaked barley or corn grits.

aerate—To mix air into a solution to provide oxygen for yeast. Brewers must aerate wort before fermentation for healthy yeast growth.

aerobic—Describes any process that takes place in the presence of oxygen. Yeast fermentation begins as an aerobic process and then changes to an anaerobic one.

airlock—A small plastic device that allows carbon dioxide to escape from a fermentation vessel while preventing air from reaching the beer inside.

ale—Typically refers to beers fermented with top-fermenting yeast strains and at higher temperatures, commonly between 65 and 75 degrees F (18 and 24 degrees C). Fermentation at higher temperatures promotes the formation by yeast of various flavor and aromatic compounds, including esters and phenols that give beer fruity and spicy flavors.

alpha acids (AA)—The chemical compounds in hops that, when isomerized by boiling, give bitterness to beer.

anaerobic—Describes a process that takes place in the absence of oxygen or that may require its absence. Yeast fermentation begins as an aerobic process and then changes to an anaerobic one.

attenuation—The degree of conversion of sugar to alcohol and CO_2 through fermentation. Beers with a low degree of attenuation will be full bodied with higher levels of residual sugar. Higher attenuated beers will be drier and lighter bodied.

blow-off tube—A flexible line of piping attached to a fermentation vessel to allow carbon dioxide and krausen to escape. *See also* airlock.

boiling—The stage of the brewing process in which wort is boiled to isomerize hop alpha acids, dissolve hop essential oils, and coagulate and remove proteins that cause haze in the finished beer.

bottom-fermenting—A reference to the tendency of yeast to flocculate at the bottom of the fermenter at the end of fermentation. Usually refers to lager yeasts.

break—The moment in time during the chilling (cold break) or boiling (hot break) of wort that causes proteins to coagulate.

caramelization—A chemical degradation of sugar through heat in which the sugar is converted to caramel. *See also* Maillard reaction.

carboy—A large glass or plastic jug, typically 5 or 6½ gallons, used by homebrewers as a fermentation vessel. Sometimes referred to as a *demijohn.*

chill haze—Suspended yeast and protein particles that give beer a cloudy appearance. Possible indication of a bacterial infection.

clarify—Any of a number of processes that remove suspended particles from beer, leaving a brighter beverage with a more vibrant color. *See also* finings.

conditioning—A period of time during which beer is allowed to mature. Conditioning imparts natural carbonation, develops flavor, and clarifies the beer by allowing suspended yeast and proteins to drop out.

decoction mashing—A traditional German process in which a portion of the grain is removed from the mash tun, boiled, and then returned to the main mash. It is used to ensure maximum starch conversion and to develop rich malt character. Modern, highly modified malts have made decoction mashing less necessary.

degrees Plato—An alternative scale to measure the amount of sugar in wort by measuring the refraction of light passing through it. A specific gravity of 1.040 equals approximately 10 degrees Plato.

diacetyl—A volatile compound produced by yeast during fermentation. While it is a desirable component of some beer styles in small amounts, in most beers, and at higher concentrations, it is generally considered a flaw. The flavor of diacetyl is commonly compared to butter or butterscotch.

diastatic power—The amount of diastatic enzyme potential that a malt contains. Diastatic enzymes break down complex starches into simpler sugars. It is through diastatic enzyme activity that brewers convert the starches in barley to fermentable sugars during the mash step of the brewing process.

dimethyl sulfide (DMS)—A compound created during fermentation with a flavor and aroma of creamed corn or cooked vegetables. Possible indication of a bacterial infection.

dry hopping—Adding hops to fermenting or conditioning beer to increase hop flavor and aroma.

enzymes—Protein-based catalysts that affect specific biochemical reactions. Diastatic enzymes break down complex starches into simpler sugars.

essential oils—The volatile compounds in hops that, when dissolved in beer, provide flavors and aromas.

esters—Aromatic compounds formed from alcohols by yeast action. Typically fruity.

final gravity (FG)—A measurement of the remaining sugar content of beer following fermentation that is based on the density of the fluid.

finings—Any of a number of ingredients added at the end of the brewing process to clarify beer. Traditional examples include isinglass, gelatin, and Irish moss.

flocculation—The state of being clumped together. For yeast, the clumping and settling out of a solution after fermentation has completed.

gelatinization—The process of rendering starches soluble in water by heat or a combination of heat and enzyme action. In making beer, the starches in grains must be gelatinized for the enzymatic conversion to fermentable sugars to occur.

germination—The stage of plant growth during which the seed puts forth a sprout. Germination is the first step in the malting process.

grain bill—The list of grains used in a beer recipe.

grist—The term for ground or milled grain prior to the mashing step of the brewing process.

HBU—Homebrew Bittering Unit. A numerical value indicating a beer's approximate potential bitterness.

hop back—A vessel filled with hops that acts as a filter, removing coagulated proteins from wort on the way to the chiller. As hot wort flows through the hop back, it dissolves essential oils from the hops that give a hop aroma to the beer.

hops—The cone-like flowers of the perennial vine *Humulus lupulus*. Used in beer, hops provide bitterness, flavor, and aroma. They also have preservative properties that can help extend the shelf life of beer.

hydrometer—A tool used to measure the density of a liquid. Sometimes referred to as a *saccharometer. See also* specific gravity.

IBU—International Bittering Unit. A chemical measurement of the actual bitterness in beer. An IBU is defined as 1 milligram of isomerized alpha acid per liter of beer. May be different from perceived bitterness.

infusion mashing—The process in which grains are soaked in water of a specified temperature for a specified period of time to activate enzymes that convert starches to sugars. The grains are not boiled. For a single-infusion mash, all of the water is added at one time and the grains are allowed to soak at a constant temperature. In a stepped-infusion mash, a portion of the water is held back and heated to a higher temperature. When added to the mash tun, it raises the temperature of the grains by carefully controlled degrees.

isomerization—A chemical process in which a compound is changed into another form with the same chemical composition but a different structure. Alpha acids in hops must be isomerized to impart bitterness in beer.

krausen—The foamy head of yeast, proteins, and hop resins that forms on beer during peak fermentation.

krausening—The practice of adding a small amount of fermenting wort to conditioning beer. The intent is to create natural carbonation through secondary fermentation.

lager—Typically refers to beers that are fermented with bottom-fermenting yeast strains at cooler temperatures, commonly between 48 and 55 degrees F (9 and 13 degrees C). Fermentation at colder temperatures inhibits the production by yeast of various flavor and aromatic compounds, resulting in beers with a crisp, clean flavor profile. Lagers are typically conditioned at temperatures near freezing for periods of weeks to months.

lightstruck—Beer that has been exposed to sunlight. Recognizable by the unpleasant, skunk-like aroma produced.

Lovibond—A unit of malt color measurement based on standardized colored solutions. Malt color is measured in degrees Lovibond. Lower numbers are lighter colored and higher numbers are darker. *See also* SRM.

lupulin glands—Small, bright yellow nodes at the base of each hop petal that contain the alpha acids and essential oils used by brewers.

Maillard reaction—A browning reaction caused by external heat wherein a sugar and an amino acid form a complex. Maillard reactions occurring during the kilning stage of the malting process yield grains that impart amber to brown color and toasty, caramel flavor compounds called "melanoidins" in the finished beer.

malt—A cereal grain, usually barley, that has gone through the malting process to begin the breakdown of starches into simpler sugars. The malting process includes germination, drying, and kilning to various degrees of color and flavor intensity. Other malted grains commonly used in beer include wheat, oats, and rye.

malt extract—Malt in the form of a dried, concentrated powder (DME) or a liquid syrup (LME) that is dissolved in water to make wort.

mashing—The stage of the brewing process in which cereal grains are steeped in water to activate enzymes that break down the complex starches into simple sugars that are fermentable by yeast. Mashing occurs in a vessel called a mash tun or, sometimes, a combined mash-lauter tun (MLT).

modification—The degree to which the starches in grain are enzymatically degraded and simplified during the germination step of the malting process. Although brewers desire highly modified malt to achieve maximum efficiency in the conversion of starches to sugar during the mash step of brewing, modification must be stopped before all of the starch has been degraded.

original gravity (OG)—A measurement of the sugar content of wort prior to fermentation based on the density of the fluid.

oxidation—The exposure of beer to oxygen. Oxidation may cause stale or cardboard flavors. In some stronger beers, the effects of oxidation can be favorable, giving a sherry-like character.

phenols—A class of aromatic compounds formed by yeast during fermentation. Typically spicy or smoky, phenols can also be medicinal. Phenols are often considered a flaw, but in some beers a bit of clove-like phenolic character is an essential part of the style.

pitching—Adding yeast to wort.

primary fermentation—The initial phase of fermentation when yeast are most active. *See also* krausen.

priming—Mixing a small amount of sugar into beer during the bottling phase to produce carbonation.

racking—Moving beer or wort from one brewing vessel to another. Also called *siphoning*.

sanitizer—Any of a number of disinfectants used to treat brewing equipment to prevent microbacterial contamination. Examples include Iodophor, bleach, and Star San.

sparge water—The water used in the process of sparging.

sparging—The process of spraying spent grains with water at the end of the mash in order to rinse out any sugars that remain when the wort is drained from the mash tun.

specific gravity (SG)—A measure of the malt sugar concentration of wort or beer based on the density of the fluid. The specific gravity of water is 1.000 at 59 degrees F (15 degrees C). Typical original gravities for beer fall between 1.035 and 1.060.

spent grains—Malt after mashing and sparging has removed its usable sugar.

SRM—Standard Reference Method. A method for measuring color in beer. Lower numbers represent a lighter color and higher numbers a darker color. *See also* Lovibond.

starter—A yeast colony grown in advance of brewing by adding a small amount of sterilized wort to it. The goal is to produce a more efficient fermentation, especially with larger batches of beer.

strike water—Hot water added at the start of mashing. Sometimes referred to as *hot liquor*.

top-fermenting—A reference to the tendency of yeast to flocculate at the top of the fermenter at the end of fermentation. It usually refers to ale yeasts.

trub—The sediment at the bottom of a fermenter. Pronounced "troob."

vorlauf—Recirculating wort through the mash or grain bed before transferring it to the brew kettle in order to enhance the clarity of the final beer.

wet hopping—Adding freshly picked, unprocessed hops to the boil or a hop back to increase hop flavor and aroma.

wort—The term for unfermented beer. Pronounced "wert."

wort chiller—A heat exchange used to speed the cooling process.

yeast—A class of unicellular fungi. During fermentation, yeast metabolizes sugar and converts it into alcohol, carbon dioxide, and an assortment of other aromatic and flavor compounds that include esters and phenols. Brewing yeasts generally fall into the family *Saccharomyces*. Top-fermenting ale yeasts are of the species *Saccharomyces cerevisiae*. Bottom-fermenting lager yeast is *Saccharomyces pastorianus*. In recent years, brewers have also increasingly begun to use a genus of wild yeast called *Brettanomyces* to produce beers with funky and sour flavors and aromas.

SOME USEFUL EQUATIONS

Alcohol by Volume

$$(\text{Original Gravity} - \text{Final Gravity}) \times 131$$

ABV to ABW Conversion

$$\text{ABV} \times 0.80$$

ABW to ABV Conversion

$$\text{ABW} \times 1.25$$

Attenuation

$$\frac{\text{Original Gravity} - \text{Final Gravity}}{\text{Original Gravity} - 1.0} \times 100$$

Homebrew Bitterness Units (HBU)

$$\text{Weight of Hops in Ounces} \times \text{Alpha Acid \%}$$

International Bitterness Units (IBU)

$$\text{IBU of Bittering Hops} = \frac{(18.7 \times \text{Weight of Hops in Ounces} \times \text{Alpha Acid \%})}{\text{Gallons of Wort}}$$

$$\text{IBU of Flavoring Hops} = \frac{(7.5 \times \text{Weight of Hops in Ounces} \times \text{Alpha Acid \%})}{\text{Gallons of Wort}}$$

$$\text{IBU of Aroma Hops} = 0$$

Add the three values for an approximate overall IBU value.

Temperature Conversions

$$\text{Degrees Fahrenheit} = (\text{Degrees Celsius} \times 1.8) + 32$$

$$\text{Degrees Celsius} = (\text{Degrees Fahrenheit} - 32) \times 0.5556$$